THE
WEDNESDAY
WORKOUT

THE WEDNESDAY WORKOUT

Practical Techniques for Rehearsing the Church Choir

Richard DeVinney

Abingdon Press
Nashville

THE WEDNESDAY WORKOUT:
PRACTICAL TECHNIQUES FOR REHEARSING THE CHURCH CHOIR

Copyright © 1993 by Abingdon Press

This book is printed on acid-free, recycled paper.

Library of Congress Cataloging-in-Publication Data

DeVinney, Richard.
   The Wednesday workout : practical techniques for rehearsing the church choir / Richard DeVinney.
      p.   cm.
   ISBN 0-687-44312-1 (acid-free paper)
   1. Choirs (Music) 2. Music rehearsals.
   MT88.D5   1993
   782.5'144—dc20   93-8285
                                                         CIP
                                                          MN

99 00 01 02—10 9 8 7 6 5 4

MANUFACTURED IN THE UNITED STATES OF AMERICA

CONTENTS

1. By the Way—You Start Tomorrow Night 7

2. Plan on Having a Good Time 15

3. Here's How: The Technical Stuff 27

4. Diction: It's More Than Just Being Understood 41

5. The Voice: Know Your Instruments 47

6. Rhythm: Is Your Music Alive? 53

7. Choice Matters 57

8. But People Always Come First 65

9. Tomorrow You Must Get Organized 77

10. What's a Choir For? 83

11. Now Do It—Week After Week After Week 89

CHAPTER ONE

BY THE WAY—YOU START TOMORROW NIGHT

W ho? Me? You want me to direct the choir at the church? You're kidding. I've never directed a choir before. I don't know anything about choir directing. I don't have time. I'm not a good enough singer. I can't play the piano. There must be someone else who could do a better job than me. The only kind of group I've ever led was a Girl Scout troop. What makes you think I can direct the choir? I can build a campfire, but I can't wave my arms in front of a group of singers. Try other people first. Try anybody. Pay somebody. Let me know if you get desperate. You are desperate? When would I start? Next week? You can't be serious? How can I possibly start next week? Can't we talk about this?

When your minister asked you to direct the adult choir at your church, you were reluctant. After you got past your disbelief and finished protesting your inexperience, the first thoughts that flooded your head as you tried to grasp the significance of this completely unexpected request had something to do with panic, right? You thought about how little you knew about the job. You haven't had any formal training in choir directing. The few voice lessons you had in college hardly qualify you to tell a whole group of people how to sing. You don't have any idea what to do with your arms in front of a musical ensemble—not to mention choosing music, and recruiting new members, and planning special programs, and keeping everyone happy. How can you possibly do it? The minister was pretty persuasive. There just wasn't anyone else. The church had to have a choir, and you were the only person who could do it, at least while they looked for someone outside of the membership who was more qualified. You agreed to try it for a few weeks, and the very day that someone more qualified than you was found, you would be eager to turn over the baton.

Well, that has all been said, but it doesn't help now. At 7:30 tomorrow night a group of curious people are going to gather at the church, and you have agreed to help them to sing something together that can be done for the congregation on Sunday. One rehearsal! How does anyone put together a choir to sing for worship in one rehearsal, especially if that person has never done it before? My assignment in this first chapter is to get you through the first night. If, after that, you are still alive and willing, the rest of the chapters will be about the rest of the times that you meet with your choir. You've taken on a challenge. But have courage. You can do it. You will survive. You won't get run out of town, at least not after the first rehearsal. Maybe after two or three, but not the first. Trust me. It won't be as bad as you think. I'll help you. Here are some ideas about getting started.

First of all, remember that many, if not most, of the singers in the choir have done it before. For the old-timers, your first rehearsal is only one of many first rehearsals in a parade of directors that goes back twenty, thirty, forty years or more. Most church choirs have members who have been in the same church, sitting in the same seats, singing many of the same anthems for fifty years. Think about it. Fifty years. And they are usually the most faithful ones, so they have been there every week for all those years. You aren't the worst director they've ever had. Regardless of your inexperience, you rank above the minister's wife twenty years ago who didn't know that the men sang lower notes than the women, or the high school boy in the 1960s who was going to show the old folks what kind of music the youth thought the church ought to have.

Can you imagine fifty years in the same choir? Does that give you a perspective that makes this one rehearsal tomorrow night a little less important? It was meant to. The veterans have seen it all before, and they and the choir will survive tomorrow night. The experience of these old hands will be helpful to you, not because you should ask them for advice, but because they have a repertoire of music that they can sing with practically no rehearsal. In fact for them, rehearsal may not make any difference at all. It might even be harmful.

Your first job is to find out what they can already do and then do some of that. What have they sung recently? For the first six weeks you will probably want to do music that they have done before, and not too long ago. So, find out what they already know. How do you do that? If there has been any systematic record keeping about what the choir has sung recently, look into it. Sometimes there's a planning calendar that also serves as a record of the choir's activities. Sometimes the date an anthem was sung is written on the card for that anthem in the library file. Sometimes it's written on the director's copy of the anthem. Sometimes there is a file of old bulletins. You will probably have to go to the church office for this. Every church does it differently, but somebody usually keeps this kind of vital information. Get your hands on some record of the worship services or the choir's work. No matter how much time it takes, do it. Make a list of the anthems the choir has sung during the last two or three years. This is an absolutely crucial first step. You must know what has been done before in order to plan the coming weeks.

As you are putting your list together, make a note of the things that have been repeated. Is there one that was done three times in one year, or four times? If so, that means the choir likes it and knows it. If it hasn't been done in four or five months, there's your first anthem. This is the way to choose the first five or six anthems you will use. You don't have time yet to worry about new music, or your favorites, or anything else except getting started. What about fitting the anthems to a particular Sunday service, with a particular sermon topic or service theme in mind? Well, we'll talk about this kind of planning later. For the first six weeks stick to general anthems of praise or prayer, or general biblical texts. Your first concern is practical. Just find music that can be done successfully and happily by the choir.

When you've picked out your anthems, you have some more questions to answer. Does the choir sing an introit or a prayer response or other service items? You discovered that when you went through the old bulletins. Again, pick out familiar things and plan them for specific dates in the next six weeks.

Now it's time to think about setup and lineup and other logistical things for your first rehearsal. Where will people sit? That's easy. Where they have always sat, for now. There aren't many advantages to the fact that choirs sing every Sunday, Sunday after Sunday, but there is one. The routine is self-perpetuating. Most of the members of the choir can come to the rehearsal, find their folders and their seats, and sing for twenty minutes before they even notice who the director is. That's what a routine does for you. It also will get the music distributed. There must be a customary way that music gets in the hands of the singers. They will have folders or slots or a librarian or some way of getting the music out and keeping track of it. Use it. You may want to improve it later, but for this first night ask somebody how it's done and just let it happen.

The time has come. Fifteen people have made it to their seats. They have some music in their hands that you picked out, and they are ready to sing. Now, be calm. Don't panic. You are in charge. Bluff for a few minutes, then see how it feels. If all else fails, be honest about your feelings. But don't apologize for being there. After all, there are reasons why each of them wasn't persuaded to direct the choir. You're doing it. So do it. Oh, yes. Two or three of the singers have already commented one way or the other on the music you picked out. Don't listen to these comments. You may very well have a complainer in the group. This person probably doesn't like more than four things the choir sings and lets everyone know about it. Don't be surprised by this, and don't let it affect your enthusiasm for your selections. Your enthusiasm is necessary. The enthusiasm of a complainer or two is not. Don't ever try to do music that you, the director, are not enthusiastic about, but don't be afraid to do things that some of your choir members don't like. I'll explain more about this later. An important thing to accomplish the first night is to get to know as many of the people as possible as quickly as possible. Pick out a kindred spirit or two. Every group—choirs are no exception—has people who are very warm and helpful to a new leader. They will ease your way if they can. They will tell you things you need to know. They will introduce you around. They will encourage you. You need one or two of these people right away, so look for them this first night. Beyond that, try to remember as many names as possible. Maybe name tags would be a good idea for the first few rehearsals. Maybe some of them don't even know everyone in the room.

Oh, by the way, as the director you do have to wave your arms in front of them. Is that a worry for you? Well, you have to do something with your arms, and directors are supposed to wave them at the singers. Usually the singers don't look up from their music often enough to see this phenomenon, but you are expected to do it. This is not a book on conducting. I'm not going to draw the usual triangles and backward capital J's to show you how to wave your arms. But I'll give you one general rule right now if you've never had anyone show you how to do this. The most important move that a conductor makes is straight down, bouncing on an imaginary rubber pad at a point just about even with the belt buckle. This move is called the downbeat. It is supposed to happen at the beginning of each measure without fail. If you don't know what a measure is, you probably shouldn't have let the minister talk you into this whole thing in the first place, but it's real important that you come straight down with your right arm on the first beat of every measure. Once you have moved your arm straight down on one, the rest is somewhat optional as long as you do the same thing every measure.

The second most important thing to know is that a singer can't sing until he or she takes a breath. The conductor must allow for this. In fact, the conductor must conduct this intake of breath. This is done with what is called a preparation beat. This is a beat generally in an upward direction that occurs one beat before the first beat on which the singers sing. (There are exceptions to this, but we won't go into them here.) Get in a good, clear preparation beat and a strong downbeat, and you're in business. The singers will then look down at their music, and you are free to do what you want until the cutoff at the end. In a future chapter I'll tell you how to get them to watch you a little more than this, and what to do if this happens. But you need to get started.

I suppose there was little point in my bringing up the conducting gesture problem because I can't solve it here. If you don't know what the conducting patterns are, you should call up someone you know who does, and have him or her show you. Then, by the way, you have to practice the patterns—a lot. The physical movements related to conducting a musical ensemble must become so habitual that you don't think about them. You will have other things that will require your attention while your choir is singing. The arm motions are just extensions of your thoughts about leading the group and about the rhythmic flow of the music. They can never be an end in themselves.

Well, we got the people in the door. They have found a place to sit. They are ready to sing. We picked out something for them to practice for Sunday. We have you started waving your arms. I guess that does it. You're on your way. Good luck. Your goal tonight in this first rehearsal goes something like this. You want to survive. Depending on how new all this is for you, you may just want to get through it without making too many obvious mistakes. That's not much of a goal, but that may be where you are. Or, your goal may be to simply get the choir ready to sing one thing next Sunday. That may be enough too. But let's suppose you're up to more than that. Maybe you want to set a more lofty goal. The best thing that could happen would be for the singers to go home after the rehearsal saying to each other, "She's going to be all right. She really did a good job for the first time." Wouldn't it be great if that happened? Let's try for that one. The real problem is that they will come back next week. We've got to get busy to get you ready for the next rehearsal. That one will be more difficult.

Each rehearsal gets harder until the honeymoon is over. You know about the honeymoon, don't you? The honeymoon lasts from the time you first walk in the door until a significant number of singers discover whether you agree with them on how things ought to be done. Keep your mouth shut for a while about anything that might be controversial. Don't let them know what you think about things like whether the choir should process in step or whether we sing too many new hymns, and try to make the honeymoon last as long as possible. A good marriage is possible if you are a fast learner, and the time to learn is during the honeymoon. Whatever the case, work hard on the first few rehearsals, and you'll have a good time after that. Choir directing is great fun. Working with singers can be as rewarding as anything you can imagine, even leading a Girl Scout troop. Be nice to the folks. Be enthusiastic. Trust them to accept you and work for you, and you'll want to have the job permanently. Good luck. I'll see you next week.

CHAPTER TWO

PLAN ON HAVING A GOOD TIME

You made it through the first week. Things didn't go too badly. The anthem didn't fall apart on Sunday. None of the singers got lost trying to follow your arm waving. Nobody has quit the choir yet. It looks like they're going to give you another chance. You've got at least one more week. What do you do now? How can you get organized so that things go smoothly for the next few weeks while you learn what you are doing? It's not as if you're going to try to stall, but you do need some breathing room while you get your act together. What should you do next? Well, the best thing you can do is make some plans—quickly.

Let's begin with rehearsal planning. If you are just starting this job, your first problem is to get going, to get a few passable rehearsals and Sundays under your belt. Long-term planning can wait a few weeks. What about the next rehearsal? And the next? You must plan carefully for every rehearsal. No matter how much experience you have, you will do no better than your planning. Time spent on getting yourself organized and making as many decisions as possible before you meet your singers is the best and most productive time you will spend. You must plan ahead in detail.

Some people are naturally spontaneous. They function best off the top of their heads. They can talk their way through anything. I know two of these people, but that's all. These are people who think on their feet, get their best ideas as they are actually doing their thing, and don't write anything down. They just do it. It's a gift. I am in awe of them, but I have no illusions that either you or I can do it that way. You and I, and almost everyone else, are only as good as our preparation when we get up in front of a group. Ordinarily, the better the leader, and therefore the better the choir director, the more time he or she puts in planning and preparation for the time spent actually leading or directing. A good choir director spends many more hours in planning and preparation than in actual rehearsal. You may not have thought about this when you agreed to take the job, but if you have any experience at all, you know it's true.

What kind of planning does a choir director have to do? Well, to begin with, someone must decide when and how often the choir is going to sing. If you believe that your congregation's tradition, the canons of your denomination, or even the Bible says that the choir must sing every Sunday, then you may not have a choice. The truth is, if you and the choir are not feeling up to singing as often as you otherwise might, there really is no rule anywhere that says you must sing an anthem by yourselves every week. Your minister may have a different idea, but if possible, take a Sunday off once in a while if that will help. Don't be afraid to let a Sunday go by occasionally without the choir singing alone. Get the folks there to lead the congregational singing, have a soloist sing, and forget about the choir singing an anthem. The congregation will appreciate the choir even more the next time they sing.

Whatever your situation, you do have to affirm that you are going to sing 52 times a year, or 40 times a year, or 382 times a year, or some number like that. Your next decision is, what are you going to choose for the choir to sing? I'll be real specific about this most important decision in a later chapter, and if you are like me, you'll spend more time choosing the music for the choir and planning which Sunday it will sing this music than any other activity. For now, just pick out six familiar pieces that you like and get started.

After you've decided when and what, the rest of your time will be spent deciding how. Let's assume that you know what you want the choir to sing. That will leave you free to think about rehearsal preparation. The first principle you must accept is an absolute. This one ought to be in the Bible. It goes like this: A choir director must never allow himself or herself to learn the music along with the choir. It is your number one responsibility to know the music *before* you put it in the hands of your singers. It isn't fair to the busy people who look to you to teach them the notes and tell them how to sing the anthem to be learning the notes or making decisions about how they should be sung during rehearsals. You will be wasting the valuable time of the singers if you haven't learned the music yourself first.

As you study an anthem that you want the choir to sing, your first job, naturally, is to learn the notes yourself. As the director, you need to know all the parts and be able to sing them. What? Do I mean you have to be able to sing to be a director? Sure. You don't have to be a soloist, but you do have to be able to sing as well as your average choir member. If you are going to be an effective leader, you must never ask a group to do something you can't do yourself. Sit down at the piano and sing all the parts all the way through. Can you do it without playing every note on the piano? If not, where are the hard parts? Mark them. What makes a particular interval or rhythmic figure hard to sing? Study the problem. Figure out how you would solve it and make a note so you can do it that way with the singers. Maybe there is an awkward skip in the tenor line. Maybe the basses have a part of the chord that they aren't used to singing. Maybe the rhythm and the natural inflection of the words don't match. The more you analyze the music and look for problems like this, the better you will be able to anticipate and hear the mistakes that the choir will make. You can focus your attention on problem sections or measures as the choir sings.

A word of caution for later, however. Just because you find what you think is a tough spot, don't correct the singers unless they actually have trouble with it. I have worked with student directors who would plan on a particular measure to be hard for the choir and would spend precious rehearsal time working on it before realizing that the singers could already do it just fine. Singers really get insulted if they are corrected for doing something wrong that they have done right. Usually, however, if you have trouble singing a measure, so will your singers, and it will help to know ahead of time, if possible, that the problem is coming. Sing, sing, sing. The more you sing it yourself, the more ideas you will get about how you want the choir to sing it and about what will tend to inhibit them from doing it that way.

Once you have the notes learned, you are ready to start thinking about how the anthem should sound as a whole. Your next consideration should probably be the text. What does the text mean? Is the anthem a "tune" anthem or a "text" anthem? Did you know that there are these two kinds? Well, it may not be a very original idea, but I think of most of the choir's music as being one or the other. An anthem that has only one word (*Alleluia*) is obviously a tune anthem. You don't worry much about whether the listener will understand the words. A setting of the "Lord's Prayer" or the "23rd Psalm" has words that are so familiar that the problem of simply understanding the words isn't very severe, though I'll have something to say about this in the chapter on diction. Anyway, for tune anthems it's important to make sure the style and expression of the singing enhances whatever text is used. It is clear that the most emphasis should be placed on the music. The words may be repetitious, or one short phrase may be used three or four times. Whatever the reason, it's apparent from studying the work that the composer was thinking more about the music than the words.

Other anthems are just as clearly text anthems. It may be an original text that says something very fresh and in a very dramatic or emphatic or inspirational way. If the words seem to be the most important element, or if they are unfamiliar to you, you need to spend considerable time studying the text. First, do you know how to pronounce all of the words, and do you know what they all mean? Get out your dictionary and check pronunciation and meaning for every word that you have any question about. Don't make up a pretty way to pronounce a word because you are singing it. Sing it the way the dictionary says to pronounce it. More about that later.

How, exactly, are you going to sustain that syllable that is de-emphasized in speech? The word *comfort,* for instance, is a big problem word for church choirs. As it is correctly spoken, the second syllable is unaccented. Technically, it is supposed to be the neutral vowel, or "schwa," which is pronounced something like "uh" and without any hint of emphasis. But your singers will resist sustaining the syllable "fort" so it sounds like "fuht" or "fuhrt" (as is approximately correct), because they tend to put too much *r* in it (especially where I work in the Midwest), and it sounds pretty ugly. So they will want to sing "fort," as in bastion or bulwark, and this is simply incorrect because it gives the syllable too much emphasis.

I bring this up not so we can debate how to sing the word *comfort,* which unfortunately we have to sing quite often in church, but so you can appreciate that there are problem words that you just have to pon-der long and hard to decide how you are going to have the choir sing them. The worst thing you can do is be surprised by the problem during the rehearsal and be asked for a decision on the spot. Count on it—you will be asked. Remember, there are only two people in my world, and probably yours, who can think of the answer every time off the top of their heads. Neither of us are one of them, so you and I had better have made this decision ahead of time. Be prepared.

Study, study, study the text. It is usually the reason the anthem has a place in the worship service in the first place. Madeline Marshall, the famous authority on English diction, once said that if the listeners can't understand what you are singing, you might as well play the piece on the clarinet. Sing the parts through and listen to yourself. How are you going to make the text understandable and expressive? That's the sub-ject of chapter 4. If the anthem is neither a tune anthem nor a text anthem (meaning neither are very interesting), you shouldn't have cho-sen it for the choir to sing. If it is both a tune anthem and a text anthem, you have a sure winner, and you'll have to work hard on both aspects.

You also must decide on the tempo. How fast should it go? Are you sure? A word of caution here. As you are getting acquainted with the choir's work, be careful not to choose a tempo for an anthem that is much slower than the choir has sung it before. As far as the singers are concerned, the right tempo is the one they have always used. If you choose a slower one, this will be pretty depressive for the group. A faster one is all right if you can bring it off. Whatever you decide, be deliberate about your choice of tempo and stick to it.

What about dynamics? Two things can be said here. First, the element of dynamics is the first place most untrained directors turn to for something to do to "polish" an anthem. We say, "Let's sing soft here and loud here," right? This is fine, but it's only one aspect of expression, so don't spend the whole rehearsal on it. Secondly, plan your dynamic levels and changes very specifically. Don't just page through the anthem with your choir, pointing out the markings. Not only can they read for themselves, but they also won't remember all your instructions if you give them all at once. Make your decisions, mark them in your score, and be insistent about them as they go by. Dynamics are the easiest element of music to work on. Not the easiest to bring off, but the easiest to communicate with your choir.

So—the right notes, correct pronunciation and understanding of the text, proper tempos, and expressive dynamics are four of the areas that need to be considered in detail before the rehearsal so you can make good decisions about them. How do you remember all this? You don't have to. It's important that you mark your score. Most directors have more or less elaborate systems for marking their music. Some use different colored highlighters or marking pens to indicate decisions they have made and reminders about the performance of the music. One color is for circling editor's marks. Another is to indicate cues for attacks. Another is for expression. You need a system. To start, just take a pencil (don't use a pen because you might want to change your mind) and circle difficult passages, words, and so on. A red pencil could indicate performance reminders for you, like tempo and dynamic changes, important cues, and problem spots. I'm not going to try to give you a system. This is a personal thing, and it will be more or less elaborate depending on how much time you have to work with it. Whatever you do, mark up your music in some systematic way. And just as important, provide a pencil for each singer and allow time in rehearsal for everyone to mark reminders in his or her own music.

You also should plan a schedule for learning and preparing each anthem you are going to use. Plan for a minimum of four weeks of rehearsals if the anthem is well known to the choir. Plan six or eight weeks if it is new, depending on how hard it is. Whatever you do, don't pick out several anthems, try them all at the rehearsal and decide then which one is in the best shape for the coming Sunday. There are two immediate things wrong with this approach. One is that new music needs time and repetition to settle into a performer's consciousness. An anthem will grow on singers, and they will feel more comfortable with it if they have sung it for several weeks. The other problem is that you won't have everybody at your rehearsal every week. If you are working six weeks ahead, a member can miss a rehearsal or two and still be familiar with the music. Be more intentional about this. Know what you are going to sing each Sunday for the next few weeks so you can plan your rehearsals.

Now, let's look at a plan for the preparation of just one anthem. Let's say you have a new piece of medium difficulty and you want to prepare it in six weeks. How might a typical plan look? Remember, this is a very deliberate plan that you have worked out, written down ahead of time, and will follow as the six weeks go by. Try to accomplish something specific each week that you can evaluate after the rehearsal is over. The plan will be different for every anthem. Here's an example:

First week: Read the music through so that the choir can get an impression of the whole thing. Then spend this week learning the most attractive part. That might be the first two pages, or the last two, or a climactic middle section. You want the choir to like the piece, so do the best part first. Get the group "into" it. That's enough learning for the first week. Now read it all the way through again, and move on to something else. Move the rehearsal along quickly, and maybe even stop before you let the choir sing the whole piece. Tell them they will have to come back next week to see how it comes out.

Second week: You will tackle the hardest part this time. Spend the bulk of the time on the section that is causing the most trouble. Review the good part that you learned last week. Then sing it all the way through again. Be enthusiastic, and keep pointing out the parts that everyone will like.

Third week: This might be diction week. After a review of last week's gains, spend your time with the text. Have them take their pencils and mark pronunciation, phrasing, inflection, and so on. Be sure to sing it through when you're done working.

Fourth week: How about working this week without the piano? It's always beneficial to sing without the piano as much as you can. Don't let the choir get any more dependent on the piano than necessary. Try the whole thing without the piano if that is appropriate. Review all that you have done before and sing it all the way through once.

Fifth week: There are still a few problem spots. Work on them. Review the notes. Review the text decisions you made last week. Work on dynamics, tone color, and expression this week.

Sixth week: Final polish. Sing with the organ. Review all details.

Every anthem needs a plan, and each one should be different, if possible. Each anthem has different problems to solve, and you want to remain unpredictable, if you can. It helps people stay awake.

Now, how about the overall order of your rehearsal? You need a plan for every minute of the time you spend with the choir. What do you think about as you decide what to do first, last, and in between? You should know what you are going to do, how long you are going to do it, and what you will do next. You may not follow your plan exactly, but you should have one. Once you have decided what order you are going to do things, write on the chalkboard or on newsprint that you have in front of the choir the list of anthems that you will work on in the order they will occur so the singers can find their music and put it in order before the rehearsal begins. This not only saves time and confusion between anthems, but it also gives the folks some confidence that you have thought about what you are going to do. It also helps them to gauge the length and pace of the rehearsal as the evening proceeds.

How long is your rehearsal? Most choirs work for somewhere

between an hour and two hours. It depends somewhat on the size of the choir, believe it or not. Your choir of fifteen singers probably won't feel like rehearsing for two hours. A lot is demanded of each person and nobody can coast for a few minutes at a time to catch their breath. A choir of forty singers allows the individual to pace himself or herself as the evening goes by, so the rehearsal can be longer. If your choir members are accustomed to one hour, stick with that until you have reason to suggest an hour and a half. When you get to an hour and a half you probably will consider a break in the middle of five or ten minutes. Obviously, this will depend on how much is expected of the choir and what the pattern has been in the past.

Let's assume that you have an hour. That isn't very much, so you'll have to be very efficient. What do you do first? Well, the first thing you should do is be at the church at least a half hour before the rehearsal. It is very important to me to prepare myself before the choir arrives. An hour before the rehearsal starts wouldn't be too much for me. Have a time of quiet in order to review your plans for the evening. You'll also need time to do the last minute things like finding music or arranging chairs or writing on the chalkboard. There is always something that needs to be done. When the first person walks in the door, you should have finished these preparations so you can give your full attention to your singers. You will then be able to make everyone feel welcome, answer their questions, meet new members, deal with problems, or just be friendly. This is what leadership is about. You are at your best when you have your own stuff done and can concentrate on other people.

Now, how do you start the rehearsal itself? Authorities differ on the importance of vocalises to warm up the singers. This subject will come in the chapter on vocal techniques, but let's assume here that you are going to do something in the way of warm-up exercises. How much time shall we allot for these? If you only have an hour, you'd better not spend more than five to seven minutes warming up. If in the remaining fifty-five minutes you need to work on six anthems, what should you think about as you decide the order? Well, the first and last choices are important. You should begin with one that the choir can sing fairly easily. It shouldn't be too demanding vocally, since you didn't warm up for very long. The best first anthem is one that is on the easy side, is chordal to facilitate tuning the choir up for what is to come, and is not the anthem for next Sunday. The last anthem of the evening should be one that the choir likes and has a melody that the singers will sing in the car on the way home. Be sure to end your rehearsal on a positive note with everybody happy about what they just sang. Do the hard stuff and the music they may not like in the middle so they will forget it until next week.

In between the first and last anthems there are other considerations to help you plan. The anthem for the coming Sunday should be carefully placed. It should come after the voices are thoroughly warmed up, all the latecomers are in their places, but before anyone is tired. That might suggest that it should be placed at about number four in a rehearsal of six anthems. Two and three should be contrasting in style and tempo, and the most difficult of the evening. This is the heavy work time of the rehearsal. These are new anthems that need lots of note pounding and that are unfamiliar and therefore still not too popular. Numbers five and six could be more or less quick read-throughs of new music for the future. If you are working on a long-range project, like a cantata, take a five-minute break and come back for another half hour. And don't forget to plan some time to go into the sanctuary and run through the anthem for Sunday with the organ.

Most church choirs have a period of devotions. Some prefer to open with these. Some have them after the last note is sung. Both times have advantages. Your choir will have to do what is best in your situation. Don't let them take too much precious rehearsal time. By the time you have devotions, announcements and business, it is hard to accomplish much actual rehearsing in the time left in the hour. Regardless of the size of your church or your choir, try to talk everyone into an hour and a half, at least. Eight anthems in an evening is a lot, but not too many to work on, so you should try to get all the time you can.

At this point you should remember that careful evaluation is a great help to future planning. Immediately after the rehearsal is over it is very important to spend a few minutes—perhaps at home as you unwind—making notes about what went right and what went wrong. Make a judgment about the progress of each piece that the choir worked on so you will know what to do with it next week. Use the notes that you have made as you plan your next rehearsal. The process of evaluation should be taken one more step once in a while. Set up a tape recorder that only you know about, and let it run throughout the rehearsal. As you listen to it after everybody has left, listen to what you do as director. Do you talk too much? Most of us do. Do you have a pleasant voice? Do you actually get the results that you ask for, or do you just make suggestions and hope? Do you sound enthusiastic? Does the choir listen to you? Do you listen to the choir, or do you sing along most of the time? This can be a very instructive exercise. It is even more helpful than listening to recordings of the choir's performance.

Evaluation is part of the planning process, and planning is the most important thing the choir director does. There are at least four kinds of planning that you must do. You must plan and prepare the rehearsal of each anthem. You must plan the order and progress of each rehearsal. You must plan the selection of music for the coming weeks, and you must plan the overall work of the choir for the year. We'll get to the long-range planning in the chapter on musical selection. Planning takes an enormous amount of time. But the more you plan, the better you will do, and the better the choir will do. And as you work, plan on having a good time.

CHAPTER THREE

HERE'S HOW: THE TECHNICAL STUFF

N
ow, let's get technical. Almost every subject mentioned in this book deserves an entire book of its own, and the technical aspects of choral singing and how they are dealt with by the conductor is one of the big ones. Unlike writing a whole book, it's pretty easy to put together a single chapter on a significant subject like this. All you have to do is pick out the most important concepts (that means those things that you actually know something about) and not worry about being comprehensive. Limited as it is to a few of my best tricks and strongest held biases, the most this chapter can do for you is give you some ideas about how to do the things that a choir director does. It is meant to stimulate your thinking and planning. It's not meant to give you a complete course in choir directing. Obviously, you will have to take some classes, attend some workshops, and read some books to gain a complete picture of how to conduct a choir. The intent of this chapter is only to get you started.

Let's begin with a little more detail about the actual gestures that you will be using in your conducting. I started you out in chapter 1 with the downbeat and its preparation. You've had a couple of weeks to try your wings (so to speak). Are you still self-conscious about waving your arms in front of the choir? Don't worry. That will go away. But don't let it go too far away. Think about it every once in a while and be objective and critical about what you are doing. One very important rule of conducting a church choir is this: Don't make your conducting movements any bigger than is absolutely necessary.

I recently heard a comment about a choir in a church nearby. The first response of the observer after she visited the church was not about the choir or its singing but about the "awful contortions" of the director. Whether the director was going through unnecessary contortions isn't what matters, but the observer was distracted to the point that she didn't respond to the singing of the choir at all. Set a goal to use the absolute minimum arm movement that will get your intended results with your singers. Ask yourself if you really want the congregation to watch you more than listen to the choir.

Having said this, let's start the positive suggestions with a well-accepted principle of conducting. Generally, the size of your arm gestures should reflect two things: the number of singers you are conducting, and the dynamics that you want them to produce. Beginning with the latter idea, it is very natural to make big motions for loud passages and small motions for soft. Be consistent, and you will gain more and more control over the voices without having to yell "louder" or whisper "Shhhh" all the time. In most churches, yelling "louder" or whispering "Shhhh" in worship on Sunday mornings is frowned on anyway. Try to communicate this direction with the relative size of your arm motions. It's also natural to make your gestures bigger for big choirs and smaller for small choirs. If you have the good fortune to conduct a choir of several groups together numbering a hundred or more singers, you have every reason to make great big motions. Nothing is more ridiculous, however, than to stand in front of twelve singers and wave your arms as high as the tallest one and sideways to the outer width of the group itself. Put all this together and it comes out like this. If you want to make great big wild motions with your arms you'd better have a choir of 200 voices in front of you singing very, very loudly. Any other time, keep the motions as small and unobtrusive as you can to get your best results. I like to deliberately test this and cut my gestures to practically nothing occasionally, or even quit conducting at all once in a while.

This suggests a good technique to use in rehearsal to help your choir members sing together more sensitively. Have them sing occasionally without moving your arms at all (and without the piano playing to hold them together). Don't do this without telling them how they are supposed to compensate for not having your leadership. Tell them that they should stick together by listening to one another. This is very good practice for them even if it does make you feel unneeded. You'll get over it.

Here are some more general suggestions for your conducting. How about your posture? Do you stand like a singer? You don't try to insist that your choir members stand up straighter than you stand yourself, do you? Posture is very important for the singer, but he or she will not do better at this than the person standing in front. Your manner, your carriage, your attitude about posture will be reflected back to you from your singers. This is just one of many things that you can communicate nonverbally to your choir. I've seen conductors stand in front of church choirs passively, stony-faced, doing little more than waving one arm and looking down at the music stand. The musical results from the singers were stiff, stilted, and uninspiring. If you have a trained professional choir of singers who have sung the music many times, you might get away with such lack of leadership as they sing. But you are directing a group of volunteer musicians of varying ability who have just learned this anthem this week. They need all the inspiration, reminders, and urging you can put together while still remembering the earlier caution about not distracting the listeners.

A big part of effective conducting is eye contact. You may complain that your singers don't look at you. Do you look at them? Why should they look up from their music if when they do they see you looking down at yours? Eye contact between conductor and singer can help the communication between them immensely. Try to know your music well enough that you can be looking at them the majority of the time. And don't sing with them. When you sing along with the choir, who's listening to see if things are being sung the way you want them to be? That's your job. Be quiet and listen.

An animated face is perhaps your greatest conducting tool. You can communicate enthusiasm and excitement, urge dramatic and passionate singing, and make your singers feel good about what they are doing just by the expression on your face. A disagreeable expression is perhaps your greatest club when things don't go as they should. It certainly beats slamming your music down and stomping out of the church. There are many subtle ways you can communicate to your singers. Your demeanor can prepare them for the mood of the music. The way you move as they get ready to sing can start the rhythmic feel of the music. Your hands can reflect the intensity or calmness of a passage by the way you hold them—either tensely or relaxed. You are like a dancer when you stand in front of a choir. Express yourself with your body, and your singers will respond almost without being aware of it themselves.

Now, let's back up to the rehearsal and look at some methods for teaching the choir an anthem. The efficiency and individual case aspects of rehearsal techniques aside, it's important to vary your approach to the learning of notes just to keep the singers alert and interested in the process. Whatever you do, don't begin the work on every anthem the same way. Don't always say, "OK. Let's start at the beginning and see how this goes," and then sing until it gets too hard to continue, stop and play the tenor part and go on until things bog down again. Use your imagination. Start at the easiest part so they have some success first. Start at the hardest part so you can solve it first before you try the piece all the way through. Start with just the melody and have everyone sing it. Start with the men or the women alone. Start by clapping a difficult rhythm problem. Start by having the singers hum while they listen to the pianist playing with them. Got the idea? Vary the approach just for the sake of varying it, not to mention that each anthem will be better rehearsed if it is approached in ways that are suggested by the music.

I was in a church choir once in which the director would quite often start work on an anthem by asking the four tenors or the seven altos to sing their most difficult part without so much as a reminder about how the thing went. The intent was to solve this one problem first before working with the whole choir. Inevitably, the singers—who, remember, are amateurs—would mess up the part, be embarrassed, and then have to work on it by themselves until they learned it. It was a really bad start for them. Before they even remembered what the music was like they were made to feel embarrassed and insecure. Give your singers a chance to get into the music before you expose them and their mistakes, and do everything you can to avoid embarrassing them in front of the rest of the choir.

As you work with your singers, don't talk too much. We all talk too much. They came to sing, not to hear you talk. Keep them singing as much as possible, and keep them busy. Keep the rehearsal moving. Pace is an important thing to understand and control. You should give the impression at all times that there is much work to be done and probably not enough time to do it. You are in a hurry, and things must keep moving. Never allow yourself a pause of uncertainty when you don't know what to do next. This is the time when you will get advice from those who will want to assist you. You can't afford suggestions from the choir members because these invariably will be off the subject and change the direction of the rehearsal. You should have planned the rehearsal so carefully that every minute has its purpose. Your fifteen singers are busy people who are giving you an hour a week, each. That's fifteen man and woman hours that you are privileged to have. Get the most that you possibly can out of every minute. That doesn't mean you won't pause for a little letdown a couple of times during the evening. But even the pauses should be planned and have a purpose. One stopping point could be a time for announcements—no more than four or five minutes. Another could be to share some family news about a choir member or concerns about someone who is sick. Be careful about stopping too long and letting the energy go out of a rehearsal. A substantial interruption of any kind can kill the momentum of a rehearsal, and sometimes this can never be regained. The minister coming in for a few jokes or items of private business with one or two members can take the steam out of a rehearsal. If she or he does this to you very often, you may have to have a heart-to-heart talk with the well-meaning pastor.

To minimize the distractions created by talking among your singers during the rehearsal, keep everybody busy. Never spend more than two or three minutes with any one section, if everyone else is sitting with nothing to do. As often as possible, when you work with one section, have the rest of the choir sing along on the part with those who are learning the notes. This will have at least two benefits besides keeping the talking down. It will help those who are needing the help by reinforcing their voices, and it will help everyone to understand the music better as they learn parts other than their own. Or, have everyone hum their own parts as one section works on its notes with the words. One dynamic you can have fun with and keep attention with in a rehearsal is good-natured competition. See who can do it better, the men or the women, the tenors or the basses. Don't ever announce the results of these competitions, just let it be good fun.

Humor is one of the best tools a choir director can use. Laughter relaxes the throat for singing. Laughter makes everyone feel good. Let the joke be on you as often as possible. Try to have at least one really funny thing happen in every rehearsal. Of course, these can't always be planned, but if there is any way to make spontaneous, unplanned, funny things happen, do it. Let the joker in the tenor section have one moment early in the evening. Then tell him that you are the one who is supposed to do the jokes and keep him from disrupting things. There's a fine line, but your singers need to have a good time. Cultivate your own sense of humor, and use it every way you can.

Back to the music. Work on small sections at a time. If you try to correct a whole bunch of widely separated mistakes at once, the singers will forget the first corrections before you get through all of them. One page at a time is enough to examine in detail, learn the notes, sing together to hear how it fits, and repeat for solidifying the gains. Here's another general principle. Don't go back and repeat a section without giving the choir a reason. To just say, "Let's start on page two and do that part again," will leave your singers wondering why. Give them a reason, even if it is one you made up just to get another repetition of the passage. After you have given one section a chance to work on a passage, fit that with one other section. The next time, fit it with a different section. Have the tenors and sopranos and basses sing their parts. Then try three sections at once. Vary this so they will hear their part in all contexts.

When the choir really needs work on the notes of an extended passage, it might be time for part rehearsals. Ask a second piano player in the group to take the men to another room to work on their parts. You stay with the women and work on the same section. This way you accomplish twice as much in a given amount of time. You could divide into four sections to work, if you have four sections and four pianists and four pianos and four rooms. Another big aid in learning difficult music is the cassette tape recorder. Sing or play each part onto a tape for each member of the choir and send these home with your singers. Some time spent at home or in the car listening and singing with the tape will teach the part in a hurry.

In rehearsal, as you are working on individual parts, have the pianist play the single line in octaves so the section that is having the problem can hear notes in an octave other than the one they are singing. By the way, here is the place to say you must give your accompanist a chance to learn the notes ahead of time. Your accompanist is your biggest asset, but he or she must have time to prepare. Never spring a new piece on your accompanist. You won't get a good accompaniment, you might embarrass your colleague, and you will waste valuable rehearsal time. Be sure your pianist has the music for next week's rehearsal this week. Also, remember that you can't afford to spend time conferring with your accompanist during the rehearsal. Anything you have to communicate exclusively to the pianist should be done before the choir arrives.

Here also is the time to plead for the piano as your rehearsal instrument. It is the best instrument for this purpose, while the organ is the worst. The piano is ideal because of its percussive nature and the fact that the player can bring out individual voices or even individual notes if that is helpful. The attack of the piano can be heard above the singing of the choir, and the singers can listen for it. The organ is inappropriate because every note sounds the same for as long as it is held. Singers have difficulty sorting out their own lines, and it holds the notes absolutely straight, unlike the way you want your singers to sing. Worst of all, the player can't help the singers by bringing out notes necessary for the choir to hear and backing off others when this is helpful. I'll say more about the organ in the chapter on rhythm, but as the director of the choir you must understand its limitations, and especially its inability to serve as a helpful rehearsal accompaniment instrument.

For this and other reasons, the sanctuary is not usually the best place to rehearse if you can help it. The sanctuary often won't have the amenities of a rehearsal room—music cabinets, adjustable seating arrangement, movable piano, blackboard, and so on. And the kind of uninhibited, informal or businesslike atmosphere that you want in a rehearsal sometimes doesn't feel appropriate in the sanctuary.

Let's talk about seating arrangements. Is your men's section small or weak? Do you find that you give too much rehearsal time to the women? Both of these problems can be helped by finding a way to seat the men in the middle or in the front. They will be taller than the women on the average, so this may be difficult unless the seating configuration is just so, but certainly in rehearsal, if only occasionally, you can put the men where they can hear and be heard more readily than in the back row.

Another seating consideration is this. If you want to be able to keep track of how each choir member sounds when he or she sings, cut down the distance between you and the row of singers that is the farthest from you. Forget about trying to duplicate the choir loft seating in your rehearsal room and arrange the choir in a semicircle in one or two rows around you. Or, try two lines facing each other or a V-shaped arrangement. Whatever you try, make sure that no singer is more than two rows away from you. You will hear better. They will hear you and one another better. They can get accustomed to hearing one another as they will sound in the choir loft when you go there to practice later in the evening.

Another good idea is to move the choir out of the loft to sing occasionally. It is good for your singers to hear themselves in other settings. If you can't arrange to sing for a nursing home or another church, move around in your own sanctuary. Sing from the back or the aisles once in a while. Sing for a church supper or a church school program. Why go to the trouble to do this? Each new place sets up different acoustical and physical experiences for the singers. They will hear themselves and one another in new ways. This can be stimulating and instructive for them. It helps to break them out of deadening habits that get firmly set if every Sunday, year after year, they sit in the same seats and sing the same way for the same listeners.

Try rehearsing sometimes with the choir members standing at arms length from one another. This will help make your singers more independent. It will encourage them to listen more carefully to one another. It will allow them to hear themselves as individuals more readily. Any change in seating or physical arrangement is good for the choir once in a while to get the singers out of their sound ruts. Moving around during rehearsal is also a good idea. Make your choir rehearsal a physical activity for everyone. Don't do all of the work yourself. It is the singers who should be getting totally involved and expending the energy. Good singing uses the entire body. But you must push, pull, plead, and persevere if you are going to convince amateur adult singers that this is true. If you let them, they will settle into their seats and just "sing along" all evening. If everyone does that, who are they singing along with?

There is a sedimentary effect at work among singers who have been choir members for a long time. As the years go by, first sopranos sometimes tend to become second sopranos, who tend to become first altos, who tend to settle in for the long haul on the second alto part. The same things sometimes happen to men. They will drop down a section when the choir is between directors so the move won't be noticed. Now this may be a good thing in some cases, but if you need first sopranos and first tenors, shake up the mixture now and then. See if you can convince some of your singers that they don't really belong on the lower parts.

One way to improve your singers' reading ability and their musicianship is to spend a few minutes each week teaching them to sing (and hear) all of the individual intervals. Start with the diatonic (major scale related) intervals from the bottom note up. Have them sing all seven—major 2nd, major 3rd, perfect 4th, perfect 5th, major 6th, major 7th and perfect 8va—by relating them to the first two notes of a familiar song. For instance, a perfect 4th is the first two notes of "Here Comes the Bride." A perfect 5th is the beginning of "Twinkle, Twinkle, Little Star." Then learn the same intervals from the top down. This is more difficult, but if your musicians can do this, they will have accomplished a very practical skill. If you get brave, have them do the minor, augmented, and diminished intervals too. Once a singer can sing the common intervals up and down, his or her sight reading will be vastly improved. When you encounter a difficult spot in an anthem, just remind everyone of the interval involved, and they'll sing it immediately.

Another way to improve the musicianship of your singers is this. Don't always give them the starting pitch from the piano. After they have been singing an anthem for a few minutes they should be able to find the pitch to start most phrases unless the music has modulated to another key. Give them time to think of the pitch, and perhaps to hum it, but don't always pound it out on the piano. Teach them to be less and less dependent on this kind of help and more and more on their own musicianship. Don't use the piano all the time anyway. The more you can rehearse without any accompaniment, the better it is for everyone, including you.

Every few weeks it is very good for your choir if you will spend fifteen minutes or so during a rehearsal to tune the sections. Good intonation doesn't just happen in a choir. Good intonation can give your choir not only a more pleasant sound, but also one that will capitalize on the matching of overtones above each note. This will fill out the sound and make it richer and more vibrant. Good intonation requires constant attention and careful listening. Take a single note on either a hum or a vowel sound and have one section sustain it while the members listen carefully. Then isolate your two best singers and have them sustain it until everyone can hear that they are in tune. Then add one or more. Keep working until everyone, including you, is listening so carefully that any variance from the pitch is heard. You will be amazed at how out of tune the casually sung pitch can be. Do this with each section. Then try a chord. The whole point is to get everyone in the room to concentrate hard on the sound. This exercise promotes careful listening during all of the singing, and it makes the singers aware of how good intonation sounds.

Another way to improve the intonation of the choir is to sing very softly. Even loud passages should be rehearsed very softly. Most people simply sing louder than they listen. It is paradoxical, but the singer can hear himself or herself better when the voice is soft rather than loud. And when singing softly, the singer can certainly hear others better. Do a lot of humming of difficult chords and passages. Intonation problems are almost always caused by lack of attention and careless listening. This is up to the director. Listen more carefully yourself, and insist that your singers listen, really listen, to themselves sing.

Don't neglect practicing the hymns for each service. Choirs (and maybe directors) sometimes take hymns for granted and decide that they can sing them better than the congregation anyway, so why waste precious rehearsal time going over them? Well, we must keep reminding ourselves that the first reason for having a choir is to lead the congregation in singing. To lead effectively, even good musicians need preparation. If we were to divide hymns into two categories, those that are familiar and those that aren't, there is good reason to work on both. Obviously, the unfamiliar ones should be practiced to make them familiar. The familiar ones make ideal material for warming up the choir. Vocalize with them to develop tone. Use the familiar harmonies to sharpen the intonation of the choir. Familiar hymns make perfect diction exercises. A little imagination and effort can pay double returns in more effective leadership in the service and better developed vocal resources in the choir.

Encourage creativity in your choir. Invite your musicians to compose music for the choir to sing. There isn't too much danger that you will get pieces you would rather not do. If you are concerned about this, ask only the best musicians and ask them privately. You probably won't get any masterpieces either, but it is good for everybody involved to have the introit on Sunday morning written by a choir member. You may be surprised at what will come from a little encouragement.

There aren't any magic tricks that will transform a group of singers into a good choir, even though most of us keep looking for them. But here is one principle that you can use that may be the best single aid to helping your choir sound better. Have your singers remember to put a slight *crescendo* on every long note that they encounter except at the end of a phrase. Most dull singing comes from the letdown of vocal energy and breath support as long notes are sung. A long note is generally a dotted half note or longer. Keep the overall singing tone alive by continually insisting on this small expansion of tone on almost every note that is sustained within a phrase.

If your singers need convincing that your suggestions will produce better results in their singing, try showing them. A picture is worth a thousand words. A demonstration is worth a thousand lectures. Don't tell them how to sing, show them. You don't need a great voice to demonstrate how you want them to sing. You can sing as well as the average singer in the choir, can't you? If you have an average voice, the average singer will imitate it more easily than if you had a great one. Show them. It's much quicker and much more effective than a lot of talk.

There is one problem that church choirs and church choir directors spend more time on than any other, even learning the correct notes and rhythms. This is the question of whether we carry over the musical line without a breath even though the music suggests a break. You've done it. You've spent hours in rehearsals debating or marking or practicing carrying over sentences that shouldn't be broken. I am writing this on Christmas Eve day, and a classic example of this universal problem is found in the most familiar carol of all, "Silent Night." You know the line. "All is calm, all is bright (most people add a period here) round yon virgin (breath) mother and child." Now are there really two sentences here with the second one beginning with "round," and are there really three people involved, a rotund virgin, a mother, and a child? Think about it. Study the words. Of course not. The whole sentence should be sung on one breath, in spite of the encouragement to breathe given by the musical line.

Choir directors need to be concerned with this important problem. We all worry about this idea of carrying over phrases because it's easy to see and it's easy to fix. Communicate it to the singers until they mark it in their music and do it. But the whole thing is really overrated as a concern, and time could sometimes be better spent on other things. There is an equally important idea that is related to it that gets very little attention. How about those places where you should break the sound when your inclination is to carry it over? In all of your choir's singing, look for spots where a short break, made clearly by the whole choir, would set apart a musical or textural phrase effectively. Often, it doesn't require a breath. The singers may not be ready to breathe. But the musical or rhythmic effect, as well as the meaning, will be enhanced greatly with a little silence. Some of our best music is silence. I don't know who said that first, but it is an important musical truth. Rests are some of our most effective musical tools.

Here's another idea. Memorizing an anthem or even a prayer response is a project that can be very beneficial to a church choir. It is not often that most choirs achieve the ideal of singing a piece of music as well as they are capable of doing. Too often we have one or two rehearsals too few to completely learn the music, and then we sing it and don't allow ourselves to repeat it for six months or more. Take time to really learn an anthem once in a while so that the choir can sing it without the music. It is a great feeling to have all eyes and minds focused together on the singing of a piece of music that everyone knows from memory.

CHAPTER FOUR

DICTION: IT'S MORE THAN JUST BEING UNDERSTOOD

Diction is worth working on frequently. You couldn't do much better than to spend half of your rehearsal time on diction. Good diction on the part of a choir will pay big dividends. Not only will the words that you sing have a better chance of being understood, but good diction also contributes to the production of a pleasant and expressive choral tone. Besides not being understood, there are many musical problems that are the result of poor diction: rhythmic imprecision, poor blend, and poor intonation are some.

Expressiveness in singing is mostly the result of proper attention to diction. Vowels carry the beauty of the voice. They must match from singer to singer for good intonation and blend. They must be correctly colored so the words can be understood. Consonants articulate the sense of the words and project it to the listener. They must be produced by the singers exactly together for clear understanding of the words and for rhythmic precision. They must be exaggerated or they won't be heard. The proper inflection is important, and to achieve it, you must study the words and how they are pronounced and what syllables are accented.

Finally, it is necessary to study each sentence to see what ideas are important to the clarity and expressiveness of the words. Does the music encourage or work against the desirable inflection of the words? Are the notes supposed to receive rhythmic stress at the same time the syllables or words are to be given less emphasis if they are to be properly understood? If so, this is a problem. You'll need to figure out a way to solve it. Once studied and taught to the choir, remind them with frequent pep talks, because diction is the first thing that amateur singers let go when they aren't thinking as they sing.

I'm going to take on the subject of diction without getting too detailed or technical and certainly without being comprehensive or complete. I'll try to give you some principles to understand and follow rather than a treatise on the individual intricacies of diction itself. Because you are just beginning your work as a choir director, you probably have neither the time nor the inclination to dig into this topic as deeply as it deserves. If you are going to be a choir director for more than six months, you must get a good book on diction and study, study, study. This subject is just as important for the choir director as anything musical. For now, I hope this chapter will get you started. Follow all of the suggestions here and you can get by for a while.

First of all, "diction" is the overall subject. All of the other terms and words like articulation, pronunciation, accent, diphthong, voiced consonant, and so on, are terms and subtopics. We are talking about the whole idea of how words are spoken and sung. It is a very complex subject. Every vowel sound and every consonant has a technical name, a symbol, and a proper way to be handled. I'm not even going to try to list or explain them. Instead, I'll take the easier route and give you broad generalizations and some key ideas. Because so much in your choir's singing depends on diction, work hard on it, and the results will be impressive.

We should begin with a philosophical statement about the pronunciation of words. I believe that all words should be sung just as they are spoken, and that the authority for their pronunciation is the dictionary. Read that sentence again. Not everyone who sings or conducts choirs believes it. Some people think that some words need to be pronounced in a special way that will make them prettier when they are sung. The word *honor,* for instance, must be made acceptable for singing by changing the second syllable to rhyme with "or." I say, nonsense. My dictionary says it's pronounced "on-er," and I say it should be pronounced that way no matter who is singing it, opera tenor Pavarotti or Elm Street Church tenor Jones.

It's hard enough for the congregation to understand what you are singing about without changing the way the words are pronounced. This principle has enormous implications, as you will see as you study the subject of diction. Please understand, I'm not talking about coloring a vowel for vocal reasons in order to sing it in the highest part of the range. Sopranos are often taught to change vowels in the direction of "ah" when they get above the staff so that their sound can be made more freely. The premise is that the ear can't tell the difference that high. I'm not going to argue with this. It's not a diction question, but a vocal production principle. The diction principle is that if words are sung correctly, they don't need to be prettied up. More about this later.

Let's get down to the basics of diction. Let's start with vowels. Generally speaking, you sustain the sound of your voice on vowels. One initial problem is that often a short or unaccented syllable in a word is set to a long or strong note, giving the syllable more importance or emphasis than it deserves. This can mess up the pronunciation, and thus the understanding, of the word. What most often makes words difficult to sing properly is what is done to their individual syllables by the rhythmic or vocal demands of the music. This is something that you have to study very carefully. Every multisyllable word has strong and weak syllables, and it isn't too hard to figure out that when the music asks you to sustain or accent a syllable that is ordinarily a weak one, you have a problem to solve. Generally, the music should give way so the word may get its proper inflection.

Begin your study of the text of an anthem by reading it aloud. As you do, check to be sure you know how to pronounce every word. Think about the meaning of the words and how that will influence the way you will sing them. Study it as poetry to see if it has unusual aspects that help it to make its point. Listen to the sound of the words.

Next, read it out loud in the exact rhythm of the anthem. See what the musical rhythm does to the words. Does it fit the rhythm of the spoken words or fight with it? A clear mark of a skillfully written anthem is one in which the music fits the words. Whatever the case, you should know what is happening in the piece you are to sing. Mark the problem spots, and think about how you will solve them. Then sing the words. Give the same emphasis and inflection to the syllables, words, and phrases that you gave when you read them. If you can do this, you're halfway home. If it doesn't work easily, you know what to work on with the choir.

Each vowel in the English language has a color of its own, and you must know what that is and how to produce it with your voice. The problem with English is that it has so many different vowel sounds. Languages like Latin and Italian are preferred by trained singers because they only have a few, pure vowel sounds. This makes them much easier to sing. First, learn the sound of the English vowels. As you teach your choir to pronounce a word in an anthem, work to get the singers to match the sound they are using with those around them. Spend a little time at each rehearsal on a specific vowel found in an anthem. Talk about how everyone should make that sound exactly alike. Have sections sing it to one another and listen. Have rows of singers match the tone color of the vowel. You may not want to get down to individual singers, but this is where this is heading. Somehow get everyone to sing the same vowel sound, and you have most of your blend and intonation problems solved.

Then come the diphthongs. These are syllables that have two vowel sounds. These are a problem. The word *high,* for instance, has two vowel sounds, "ah" and "ee." The problem comes when you try to sustain the word. Which sound do you hold, and for how long? The general rule is, sustain the first sound, in this case, "ah," with no hint of the second until the last instant. Singers will usually try to fudge this rule by sliding into the second too soon and produce some mixture of the two sounds. Singers in some areas of the country or some styles of music will go immediately to the second sound, ready or not. There are very few words where this is appropriate, one being "few," which is an "ee" followed by an "oo." The second is the one you sustain. See how complicated it gets? Let's not try to get too far into it. You can get along pretty well with diphthongs if you insist that your singers hold the first sound purely and clearly and with determination, and slip in the second at the last possible moment.

Now, while we are on this subject, we'll take it one big step further by considering the ugly *r* that spoils so much singing. Nothing will do more damage to the sound of the human voice than any attempt to sustain an *r*. People try to make a diphthong out of a vowel and an *r*. Example—the word *Lord*. The vowel is "aw." Now, if you sing "aw" and move too soon to an *r* you will create a guttural sound that will spoil the whole anthem. And we have this problem all the time in the church. How often do we sing, "Lord," "Word," "Mercy," "For," and so on. All these words have this terrible trap in them. You will have to spend a lot of time and energy reminding your singers about this one. Pure diction people say without equivocation, don't sing the *r* at all. That is how serious this problem is. You may not want to go that far, but you must get as much of the *r* out of the sustained sound as you can. It is deadly.

Then, there are consonants. Here's the big idea about consonants. Vowels have to be sung. Most consonants do not, and when they aren't your choir's singing is mush. Let me explain. If your singers don't produce vowels, there won't be any sound. They have to produce vowels because the sound of their voices rides on the vowels. But they don't have to sing most consonants audibly at all. They will think they are singing the consonants audibly. They will go through the motions with their tongues and their lips, but most consonants don't last long, some don't have any tone at all, and none will be heard unless they are exaggerated.

Consonants are very important. The rhythm of the music depends on the consonants your singers produce. Each *t* and *d* and *s* must be produced at exactly the same time, and that time must be in precisely the right place in the measure to produce intelligible rhythm. The real problem for amateur singers is that the clear, precise, and exaggerated production of consonants is not only dependent on careful rehearsal, but also on energy and motivation. Lazy, thoughtless, routine, habitual singing will turn out sloppy and unheard consonants without fail. You must not only practice the articulation of consonants diligently, you must also give pep talks, sermons, bribes, threats, and reminders to your singers every Sunday, or they won't put forth the energy and thought required. Well-trained singers develop habits of good articulation. Volunteer church choir singers sing too much music, too often on too little rehearsal time to develop very many reliable habits in this area. You just have to keep at it, every week.

Again, this is a very complicated subject. There are voiced consonants and unvoiced consonants. There are initial consonants and final consonants. There are hard consonants and soft consonants. On long notes, getting to the *r* or the *l* too soon can completely spoil the sound of the word, but getting to the *m* or the *n* a little early can make it beautifully expressive. Get yourself a good book on diction and study consonants. Their treatment is vital. For now, plead with your singers to follow your well-rehearsed demonstrations of energetically produced consonants that are precisely placed on specific beats of the music, and you will improve the sound of the choir tremendously. The more work you do in this area, the greater will be the rewards. There are people who listen to a choir and all they care about is whether they can understand the words. If, after a Sunday or two, somebody comes up to you and says that they understood every word, you may have received the highest compliment that a person can give. But it won't happen unless you spend considerable time working on diction.

CHAPTER FIVE

THE VOICE: KNOW YOUR INSTRUMENTS

The study of the voice and how to improve its tone is extremely difficult to deal with in a book of words. The first problem, of course, is that the subject is sound, and these pages don't make much sound unless you turn them vigorously or drop them on the floor. Sound is subjective by its very nature, and writing about it is an exercise in imagination at best. Furthermore, the sounds you and I produce with our voices are made and controlled with more involuntary muscles than voluntary ones, so our control over our voice is in many respects a secondary function to some other function of our body. And the voice is dependent on the participation of the entire body doing things that we ordinarily don't ask it to do.

Taking voice lessons is a real good idea for a choir director. You should know as much as possible about the instrument that you are asking your musicians to use to make music. But watch out. There are more unqualified voice teachers out there taking money for their services than qualified ones, and you must choose your teacher with care. And if you find a good one, you must have a good rapport with him or her in order to work with confidence. She or he must have a very good ear and a thorough knowledge of vocal techniques and how to teach their mysteries to the singing student. Obviously, you will not get in this chapter a comprehensive lesson in how to train your own voice or the voices of your choir members. The best you will get are some ideas and suggestions. What you read here will be simplistic and subjective. The benefit you gain from the reading will depend on your awareness of what is going on in your own body when you sing, on how closely you listen to the sounds that are made by your voice and the voices of others, and on your ingenuity in applying some general principles that may or may not be helpful in all cases.

If you can't take private lessons, here's something you might be able to do that would be very helpful. Recently, I attended a workshop on the Alexander Technique. The application of some of the principles of this study have done more for my own singing voice than a lifetime of interest, experimentation, and training. The Alexander Technique is not new, it is not a fad, it is not a radical point of view. It is a method of positioning and moving the body to enable it to function in the most efficient manner. Alexander teachers are on the staff of world famous conservatories, acting schools, and opera houses everywhere, helping performers of all kinds to be their best. If you have a chance to take an Alexander class, don't let it go by, regardless of your level of knowledge or experience in singing. It could change your life.

The production of a pleasant, well-resonated, natural sound by the voice begins with good posture. You've heard this before. You've dealt with it before. This is because it is true. Maybe you need to think again about why it's true. Remember, the way that a good singing voice is produced is that energy is generated in the form of air deep in the lungs, and driven upwards toward the larynx, or voice box containing the vocal bands. As this air passes over the vocal bands it causes them to vibrate, which produces sound. From there, everything depends on these sounds being resonated by as much open and relaxed space as the singer can provide in his or her throat, mouth, nasal and sinus cavities, and any other space available. And this depends on the absence of tension, anywhere above the voice box. If your choir members could just avoid interfering with this resonation by failing to open the throat or by allowing tension in the neck or face or tongue or any of the other body parts that get tense, they would sound like opera singers. And the first principle is that the production of breath and the releasing of tension are both initially dependent on proper posture. Then the problem is that all attempts to free up the sound to resonate openly are made more difficult by the work that the tongue, mouth, and lips have to do to articulate the words. Changing the shape of these articulators creates tension and inhibits the tone. To make matters worse, most of the tension is so common that the singer isn't aware that it is there.

After you understand all this, you should spend some time in every rehearsal trying to develop good habits of tone production in your singers that will enable them to let their natural voices be heard. The best sound that a voice can make is the freest and most natural one. You must try to create muscle action, tension, and energy in the abdomen to push and control the air's movement from the lungs, and then release any tension from the neck up.

Let's start again. Breath control is vital, and most people, left to their own bad habits, will inhale upside down. Ask them to take a big breath, and they will lift their shoulders and pull in their abdomen. This, of course cramps their lungs and prevents a full breath from being taken. Urge them to keep their shoulders quiet and let the air fill up their chest cavity and spill downwards as far as possible. Once full, their lungs can supply the large amount of energy and wind needed to make the voice sound. As the breath surges upward, the only resistance it should encounter is the small opening of the larynx. The two vocal bands will lengthen and shorten to create the pitch of the sound, which will then move outward to be shaped and resonated. The singer must shape it as a vowel sound with tongue, mouth, and lips, and articulate it with consonants using tongue and lips. It's a simple process, but it's not easy.

For most people, the problem is the breathing part and the tension. Whenever you do vocalises with your choir, include some breathing exercises. Try to get good habits established. Talk about breath all the time. Here's an important point. Allow time for the singers to inhale before they start. Remember the preparation beat that you are going to include in your conducting gestures? Get in the habit of pointing out the preparation beat as a time to breathe. For example, if you are rehearsing a passage in which the singers are to start on the first beat of a 4/4 measure, you might say out loud, exactly in the tempo you want them to sing, "one," "two," "sing," with the word *sing* coming on three. Have the singers use all of the fourth beat to breathe in and then attack the note on beat one of the first measure. Putting the initial inhalation precisely on a beat is often a good idea. Unless you continually insist that your singers think about breathing in, they will not think of it in time to take in enough breath to produce a good tone when they do sing. And, as the music proceeds, always talk about bigger breaths. Shallow breathing is a habit for everyone, and it is the bane of good singing.

Let's deal here with vocal exercises. The first thing that most singers expect of their new director is that the rehearsal will begin with some exercises that will require them to sing nonsense syllables in some strange fashion so that they will make fools of themselves. The only thing that saves this experience is that everyone in the room is required to do it, so nobody feels self-conscious. Should you start your rehearsal with some vocal exercises? Sure. You want the singers to think you know what you are doing, don't you? But what purpose is served by five or ten minutes spent in warm-ups?

There are lots of reasons to use vocalises. Here's a partial list:

1. Warm up the voice. These people haven't sung all day. Most of them have talked a lot, but they haven't used the full range of their voices. They need to get their singing muscles warmed up.

2. Proper breathing. Without having to think of notes or words, they can concentrate on your suggestions about how to breathe.

3. Relaxation. Use exercises that will encourage the release of tension everywhere—back, shoulders, neck, face, tongue, throat. Tension is the greatest enemy of good singing.

4. Range extension. Every week you should ease the voices higher and lower with good, open resonance.

5. Agility. Practice fast exercises so that the singers will develop their ability to control their voices along quick passages.

6. Intonation. Do some soft humming or singing while everybody listens carefully for good intonation. Singers can hear it if they make it a habit to listen for it.

7. *Vowels.* Sing some vowel sounds and insist that everyone produce these exactly the same way. Careful listening is the key here, too.

8. *Consonants.* Do some fast word exercises to wake up the articulators in the face. Talk about exaggerating the consonants.

As you do these exercises, talk often about posture. To help your singers develop good habits in this area, try to differentiate specifically between singing posture and resting posture. Demonstrate that there is a difference and insist that they move from one to the other as they work and rest. Adults really prefer to settle into a way of sitting for the entire rehearsal that they think will pass for "sitting up straight," but which is also comfortable enough to doze off if the rehearsal gets boring. Instead of just prodding them to sit up all the time, suggest two different ways of sitting. Then, the resting position will be acceptable at times, but clearly not at others.

If you are a trained singer, a good way to strengthen your choir vocally is to start a voice class. For thirty minutes before the rehearsal each week, offer to give specific and concentrated training in vocal production to all those who are interested. Limit the time to six or eight weeks so people can see the end of their commitment, and then do it again in a couple of months if there is interest. You will probably be surprised at how many will be eager for this kind of help. You can accomplish a great deal in this way that can't be done in rehearsals.

If you are not a trained singer, invite a good voice teacher to come on a Saturday morning or some other time and give a group lesson to your singers. You could do this twice a year, and then refer to what they have heard during the intervening rehearsals.

Singers are performers who play instruments. The instruments are their voices. Just like the violin or the clarinet, the singer needs to know how to make his or her instrument sound its best. One way or another, you as the choir director need to find ways to help in this process.

CHAPTER SIX

RHYTHM: IS YOUR MUSIC ALIVE?

T his won't be a long chapter. It's included mainly because church music is too often dull, and what's missing from a lot of the music we all produce in worship is the life and vitality and energy that comes from precisely, enthusiastically, and insistently performed rhythm. Let's start with five rhythmic ideas.

1. Sing with joy and vitality. Just because we're in church doesn't mean that the music has to be slow, soft, solemn, and boring. I don't hear any arguments about this one. It's hard to imagine anyone arguing that worship should be quiet and somber all the time, but too much of our music comes out that way. Many church choirs even look that way. Start bringing some life into your choir's contribution to the service by having some fun with your singing. Get your singers to smile, to look like singing is a pleasant experience. Many people give the impression that singing causes some kind of mysterious pain in their faces. It's also possible that if you could hear them singing by themselves they would cause a similar pain in your ears. Singing is fun. It should look like it and sound like it. Worship is a pleasant experience. The sanctuary is a place where all emotions are appropriate, even pleasure and joy. Let's produce music that uplifts, that has vitality, that causes people to smile once in a while. The best place to start is with the rhythm.

2. Accent the beat. The organ may be the instrument of choice for worship because a lot of sound can be made by one person and because it sounds "churchy," but it doesn't have to anesthetize everyone with unending, unrhythmic droning. Now, don't get me wrong. I'm not against the organ. I have spent more of my life sitting on an organ bench than just about anywhere else other than my bed. But the organ is such a terrible tempter. It is so easy for an organist to find a beautiful sound with just the right stops and just the right harmony and then just hold on to it until he or she finds another beautiful sound. For too many organists, music begins with the sound of the stops, progresses with beautiful melodies, and then rests quietly and fairly motionless on pleasant harmonies. Rhythm as a basic element of the music isn't really considered an expressive or dramatic tool, just a means of holding everything together.

The truth is, vital music isn't just beautiful sounds. The beautiful sounds must be brought to life with rhythm. And the organ is the least rhythmic of instruments (along with the harpsichord) because it doesn't have the capacity to accent. Every note in a phrase on the organ has the same strength as every other note. The organist can't emphasize the first beat of the measure in traditional ways because it just isn't possible. This is why organ music can sound so lifeless. Our Western music is organized or made metrical by means of stress or accent. The first beat is accented, another beat is next in importance, another next and another least. The organist must produce the illusion of accent with little tricks, since he or she can't do it directly. A note will sound more important than others around it if there is a little silence just before it, or if it is ornamented, or if it is longer or higher than the others or is reinforced by a chord. All of these tricks are available to the organist, but they have to be exploited if organ music is to come alive. As choir director you might find ways to encourage any organists you work with who don't understand this fundamental principle.

Music must have rhythm. Rhythm is given its life by its pulse or beat. The beat must be communicated by accent. The organist must find ways to create the illusion of accent now and then if the music is to have a rhythmic pulse, and the best way to do this is with a tiny bit of silence before and/or after important notes. Organists spend the first two years of their training learning to play *legato* and the rest of their lives learning when not to. The latter is the part that many of them miss.

3. Strive for rhythmic precision. The rhythmic cure for static, uninteresting music is not necessarily faster tempos. The hymns may be too slow, but that in itself isn't the only reason the congregational singing is dull. Still with me? Lively and vital rhythm doesn't depend entirely on tempo. Tempo is certainly important, and good, brisk tempos help the singing of hymns and anthems immensely. But tempo isn't everything. If you want to liven up an anthem, you must do more than just speed it up. Rhythmic precision, as produced by the consonants that your singers sing, is just as important. You must train your singers to sing eighth notes exactly even, sixteenth notes very clearly, and dotted notes just the right length. You must practice and practice until attacks and releases are precisely together and precisely on the correct beat. Releases should come on a beat of your choice, but everybody must do it. Rhythmic accuracy is crucial to the life of the music you sing. Too many choirs just sing on and on with long chords and no sense of the rhythmic activity that is also in the music, and their congregations spend the anthem time catching up on their reading or their daydreaming. Pretty harmonies are good for a couple of lines, but after this they simply soothe the ear like a warm shower soothes the back muscles in the morning before the real activities of the day begin.

4. Break up the music with proper phrasing. Little pieces of silence are desperately needed to make music alive and interesting in the church—and everywhere else. We all need to work harder on phrasing. The rhythmic life and the energy of a piece of music can be stirred tremendously by a few carefully placed and performed breaks, sometimes in places that are unexpected. Look through the text of each anthem and see if there are commas that suggest an effective place to have every voice break the sound for an instant—not long enough for a breath, just for an instant. A quick, clean break in the tone can often do wonderful things for the expression of both the text and the music. Silence is golden. A little of it can make an anthem glow with new and more colorful beauty.

5. Feel the pulse. Rhythm is the lifeblood of music. The beat is its pulse. Check your worship music. Is there a pulse? Spend time in rehearsal doing rhythmic things. Clap rhythms. Get everybody up and have them walk or march around as they sing. Talk about rhythm all the time. Everything that happens in a piece of music should happen at a specific and exact time. And in music, time is measured in terms of rhythm. Everything is related to the beat or the part of the beat on which it falls.

How do you teach the rhythm of an anthem to your choir? Well, this one isn't easy. You probably attack this from several directions. First of all, the singers in a group will imitate the rhythm patterns that they hear, either from the piano or from other singers or from demonstrations by you. Learning by rote isn't bad. If the pianist is very clear about the rhythm that he or she communicates, the choir will pick up on it. You as the director must be alert to rhythmic errors and correct them. It's OK to admit that most of us learned most of what we know about rhythm by singing or playing in a group where we imitated what we heard other people doing. This certainly is the way to begin.

But you should be more intentional than this several times in each rehearsal, too. Give your musicians little lessons in note values and meter signatures and counting and rests whenever a rhythm problem comes up. Don't be afraid to step to the chalkboard and be a teacher when it comes to rhythm. Most of your singers would really like to understand the mysteries of rhythm, and they will be very attentive. Over a period of time, the little lessons will pay off.

Beyond that, just be very specific about the rhythmic aspects of the music you work on. In order to produce precise attacks and releases with the choir, you must talk about what beat these fall on. Make the language of rhythm a part of your language as you direct a rehearsal, and your choir will learn. Rhythm is a fundamental aspect of musicianship, and as your singers learn to work better with you, rhythm will be one of the elements that will grow in their work.

CHAPTER SEVEN

CHOICE MATTERS

A s was pointed out earlier, one of the first things you have to do as a new choir director, and as an old choir director, is pick out music for the choir to sing. This is a difficult job. Not only does the successful performance by the choir depend on music of the right difficulty for its capability, but also the appropriateness of the musical contribution to the service is vital to the worship of the congregation. There are many considerations that can affect your choice of music. And what you choose will reflect your tastes and abilities, which will affect how your people react to you as a musician. The first thing choir members talk about when they get a new director is the kind of music he or she asks them to sing. The first thing that members of a congregation say about a new choir director is "yes, they do," or "no, they don't" like the music he or she chooses for the choir. What the choir sings is clearly as important as how it sings, and your responsibility as the director to choose the music is as important as anything you do.

What do you have to think about as you look through the choir's library or through the stacks of new music that come in the mail? Many things will go through your mind. Some are of absolutely vital importance. Some are secondary. Here are some of the things you should consider. First comes the obvious question—do you like the piece? Will the choir like the piece? Music is supposed to be attractive, and its purpose is to enhance, beautify, and intensify the text that contains its message. Now, one of the problems when considering whether the choir will like the music is that your diverse group of musicians includes widely varying tastes and preferences. What some of your singers will like, some others won't. It's inevitable.

Two things are very important as you consider all this. The first is that there is one person who absolutely must be enthusiastic about the piece. That person is you. The director must like the music, or its performance won't be very successful. The other important thing is that you must choose as wide a variety of music as you can within the boundaries of your own taste and what is appropriate for your church. A choir member won't mind singing an anthem he or she is not especially fond of this Sunday if there is a good possibility that next Sunday an anthem will come along that is a favorite. Everyone must get a good one on a regular basis or choir won't be fun. There are very few pieces in this world that everyone will like. Trust me. One will come along once in a while, but don't spend too much time looking for it. Look for things that you like, and that the people will like who didn't like the one you chose last week. I sometimes figure that I'm trying to keep everyone in the choir just a little bit unhappy about my choice of music. That way everyone will be real close to being happy all the time.

Your second consideration will probably be practicality. If you have a choir of fifteen, with twelve women and three men, you probably shouldn't decide to do Handel's *Messiah* next year. You must be realistic about your choir's ability. This is where you try for a balance between pieces that are too easy, producing little satisfaction for hard work and accomplishment, and those that are too difficult, producing much confusion, frustration, and unsuccessful singing even after many rehearsals. One principle is important to remember. If the choir can sing it through correctly the first time, it probably isn't worth working on. There will be few rewards for so little effort. Be realistic, but don't shortchange your choir. Given the considerations of choir size and experience, another general principle is that people can do anything you can teach them to do. Don't think that all of your practical limitations come from the choir. Don't be afraid to challenge yourself and them. That is the only way you and the choir can grow.

The next consideration is appropriateness. Does the anthem contribute something to the worship service of the day? This is a difficult one. You may be working with a minister who doesn't choose a sermon topic or worship emphasis more than a week ahead of each service. You have to prepare music six weeks ahead. How can you possibly choose appropriate music for a service yet to be planned? Every situation has its own solution to this problem, and you must work at it in both directions. You must continually lobby for earlier planning. I have worked with ministers who plan a year ahead—sermon topic, scripture readings, and hymns. What a luxury. I planned a year ahead too. I have worked with ministers who do their planning on Friday—that's the Friday before the Sunday in question.

Fortunately, there are things you can count on. The first is the season of the year. Advent will come when it is supposed to come. So will Lent. So will holiday Sundays. The church year is a sure guide that you can use. A lectionary being used by your preacher is another. On the other side, a fairly large percentage of anthems you might choose are appropriate for almost any Sunday. Many are anthems of praise or prayer that have no specific reference in the text. You can choose the majority of your anthems with these two things in mind. The Sundays that you and the minister come together with just the right topic and music may not happen very often, but keep trying. They will happen occasionally. Try to stay flexible. Have six or eight anthems going at all times. Keep your ears and eyes open, and make switches when it will help. Appropriateness is difficult to achieve on a regular basis unless everyone involved in worship sits down together regularly and plans at least a couple of months ahead. And when you mix in all the other considerations that I'm bringing up, choosing a perfectly appropriate anthem is tough.

Here are some more suggestions. How about the text itself? This is where I always start. If it isn't from Scripture, or wasn't written by an established poet, hymn writer, or theologian, is it a good text for your choir to sing? Do you believe what it says? Do you think it contains an appropriate emphasis for your denomination or congregation? When I talk with ministers about the theology of the hymns they choose or the anthems the choir sings, I like to point out that I am trying to be consistent with the language and emphases that I hear from the pulpit. The favorite hymns of the older generations may very well be about things that the minister doesn't talk about or even wants the congregation to be thinking about if he or she would admit it. The texts of your anthems should be strong, biblical, fresh-sounding poetry that everyone can affirm.

Your next consideration should be the music. Do you like it? Does it have some originality? Does it have a climactic moment and a good ending? Musical taste is subjective, but it is your responsibility to anticipate how the music will be received both by the singers and the listeners. Variety is important, not only because there are varied tastes among your people, but also because the development of musicianship and taste among those same people is one of your jobs. Sing music from all periods of musical composition, not just your particular favorites. A responsible director will continually try to educate singers and listeners about good music and gradually do more and more music that has intrinsic value of its own as the weeks go by. Two other concerns should be mentioned. You also have to consider requests. This can get a little difficult at times. And you must consider how long it has been since the anthem was used.

I spend hours and hours, weeks and weeks, all summer, every summer trying to choose music for the choir to sing. I spend way too much time. I look at every piece of music in the choir's library every summer. (That's a good idea.) I also look through hundreds of new anthems that I get from publishers and from a lifetime accumulation in my personal reference library. (I think this may be a waste of time.) I've always done this, but I'm at the point where I think I should quit. There must be a better way to find new music. I think hundreds of composers of church choir music are all writing the same anthem these days. They all seem to sound the same. I went to a publishers' workshop several years ago and sang through the selections of new music by some well-known composers. This may be hard to believe, but every single anthem we sang in the four hours was in 4/4 time, pop style. And almost every melody started after an eighth rest.

It may be that the best way to find new music is to find out what other choirs are doing. Make friends with other choir directors and ask them what their best anthems are. Go to workshops and conferences not sponsored by publishers, and ask everybody you see. When you run out of money for new music (if you have any money for new music) dig through the cantatas and oratorios in your library for individual anthems to use. Sometimes you can find some very good things that you ordinarily wouldn't think about. Be careful, though. Don't try to do things that are too big or difficult for your choir.

I have a tool for choosing music that I've used for years, and it has been very helpful. I use a system of voting that allows every choir member to register a reaction to each anthem after he or she has sung it with the choir. They express this reaction in a numerical rating, and then I average the numbers. Each anthem gets a score, and I have a tangible guide to use as one consideration when I decide next time whether to use that anthem. This is how it works.

When the choir returns to the choir room after the worship service on Sunday it is time to turn in the anthem that was sung for the service. I have four slots for them to put the music, but they could just be piles on a table. The four are labeled "4," "3," "2," and "1." Four means the anthem is a favorite. Three means it's a good one. Two means it's OK, but not much, and one means forget it. I tell the choir that their rating should have nothing to do with how well we sang it, just with their own reaction to the piece itself. I count up the number of fours, threes, twos, and ones, and then produce an average, carried to two decimal points like a baseball batting average. A 3.85 would signify a very well-liked anthem. A 2.05 would be one that few people enjoyed very much.

I tell the choir members that this isn't going to determine whether we ever sing the anthem again, but I sure do use the rating as one factor in making future choices. It is interesting to see whether the rating of an anthem goes up or down the second time it is sung. I post these ratings for everyone to see, and have discovered that another benefit comes from this. Those who don't like a piece will often see that most other people do. It's very instructive for everyone concerned, and it even helps to get used music collected so it won't clutter up the folders.

Here's another planning tool, that is also very helpful in choosing music. During the summer I always draw up a chart for the year on heavy posterboard, six months on each side. Across the width of this large card I have a long slot for each Sunday, about three quarters of an inch high. Then I draw columns from top to bottom for such things as the sermon topic for each Sunday, the hymns to be sung, the day of the church year, the anthem, responses the choir will sing, the solos or anthems by other choirs, the organ music, and special programs. I fill in the information that I'm not responsible for whenever it becomes available. I spend the summer filling in as much of the information that is mine to plan for the entire year. I do it all in pencil, and as the year goes by I change most of it. But I have something to change from, and most changes are in the form of rearrangements. Very often the best selections of music are made way ahead of time. Looking at a chart like this you can easily see how you are doing in balancing the needs for variety in style and difficulty, new and old, accompanied and unaccompanied, and all of the other things that you must juggle as you choose. Then the card becomes an easy-to-read permanent record of what we did last year and every year.

As you look for variety, do you always stick to four-part anthems by the choir? How about an occasional day off for the men while the women sing something by themselves? Then switch. How about using instruments as often as possible? How about looking through the hymnal for hymns that can be sung as anthems? This is a good way to save money, when you don't have much for new music. Most hymnals have material in them that no one has discovered yet, and sometimes these things can be turned into wonderful anthems.

Maybe these words on choosing music for the choir should have begun with this question: Should the director have the only say about what the choir will sing? I've been directing church choirs off and on for more than thirty years, and I've never allowed anyone to help me pick out the music the choir will sing. I've kept the decision making all to myself. Maybe that's wrong. Maybe I should have a committee. Maybe I should let the choir vote. Maybe I should ask the minister or my wife or someone else to help. . . . Nah. I couldn't do it. It's a truism that the best choirs are dictatorships, and here is one area where I hold absolute control. If you are willing to accept the responsibility, you probably should stake your success as a choir director on your own choices of music. If you do this, you'd better make sure you give it very careful thought. Choice matters—to everyone.

CHAPTER EIGHT

BUT PEOPLE ALWAYS COME FIRST

So, you really are a beginner? If you are, it's time we tackled the really tough part of being a church choir director. Are you ready? Here it comes. This chapter deals with a subject that has caused you some concern as you consider your future as a choir director. If it hasn't troubled you, it should. You can be the best singer-musician-director in your county, but if you can't get along with the people in your choir, if you can't motivate them, keep them happy, guide them in their relationship to the worship of your congregation, you won't survive more than three and a half weeks in the church choir business.

Time and again I have seen fine musicians fail in church work because they didn't know that, unlike other musical places, the music doesn't come first in the church even for those like you who are charged with the responsibility for making it. The people come first. If you think for one minute that as choir director your number one responsibility in the church is to produce music, you'd better volunteer for a job as a snowplow operator or an airplane pilot somewhere. Those jobs can be done successfully by persons with no people skills at all. Church choir directing cannot. Your first responsibility is to lead, serve, love, motivate, counsel, teach, support, care about, and direct a group of persons who have a wide variety of needs and who just happen to like to sing. Your second responsibility through all of this is to get these persons to sing together for worship. This is a fundamental truth for church musicians, and you need to understand it before you walk in the door.

This, of course, is both good news and bad news. The people that you work with are the best part. When most people sing, especially nonprofessional musicians, they often pour their hearts into their music. They respond to good music and good singing with unbridled enthusiasm, and they are readily moved by the powerful, spiritual moments that happen when they sing for worship. The people of your choir will love you, support you, help you, nurture you in more ways than you can imagine if you are good to them. They love to sing, to sing successfully, and to be rewarded for their efforts by kind words from you and the congregation. Praise them often and do it publicly. Urge your minister to praise them publicly. They are giving more time to the work of the church than perhaps any other lay people. They are serving in a very important capacity, and everyone must let them know they are appreciated. They will respond to this and to you, and you will be glad you made the effort.

But they also may cause you some discomfort. As you work with them, you must understand as much as you can about the people who sit in those seats in front of you. Look at them. Listen to them. Try to get behind what they say to you and understand why they behave as they do. A choir director must be a good amateur psychologist. That's a rule. And the first thing you must understand about your people is what it takes to be a singer in the first place.

Think about it. When a person opens his or her mouth and sings in front of another person, or worse yet a group of persons, he or she is being exposed to judgment, ridicule, and rejection more readily than with almost any other activity. As you get to know singers, you will see more ego and insecurity in them than in any other kind of musician. Surely, I exaggerate, right? Maybe. But after you've worked with a few hundred singers over a period of years, let's talk about it again. Singing is a very threatening activity for the person with the slightest bit of inse-curity. And who isn't at least a little bit insecure? When I stand in front of a group of people and sing, I am vulnerable to their judgment about my voice, my musical ability, my sincerity, my appearance—everything that a public speaker has to deal with, and the added dimension of the beauty or lack of beauty of my voice. It is a terrifying activity. If you have not done it, you must try to understand.

The implications of this for the volunteer church choir member are enormous. He or she is putting this on the line every week for approval, affirmation, support, and encouragement. Some people offer their voices to the choir timidly, some apologetically, some with confidence, some with arrogance, some daring you to criticize, some wanting you to criticize, some oblivious to criticism, and some devastated by it. Some will be personally crushed if you don't acknowledge and praise their singing. Some will be embarrassed if you do. Some will be hurt or mad if you don't ask them to sing solos. Some will be terrified if you do.

If all this is daunting to you as you begin working with your singers, don't worry about it, just think about it. You can't lie awake nights worrying about each person's reaction to every little thing you say and do. But do try to understand where the reaction comes from, and the first place it comes from is the unique place that singing has in the personal psyche.

Notice as you get into this business how often the way a person sings is a reflection of his or her whole personality. This is particularly true of a soloist. Aggressive, confident, outgoing people will usually have big, loud, wide open, often undisciplined voices and will sing with little rehearsal and without holding anything back. Quiet, timid people will have thin little voices and will require your constant encouragement to sing to anyone past the second row of pews. Precise, highly organized people will plan every note they sing, will rehearse as often as they possibly can and won't open their mouths unless they are absolutely sure of every detail involved in what they are going to do. It is fascinating to observe this in people, and helpful to you if you are going to know how to work with singers each week.

There also is a whole range of nonmusical needs that your choir members have that will affect the way they participate in the choir. Most people are a joy to work with in the church, and most will respond to your love and enthusiasm with an equal or even greater amount. Working in the church is one of the most exhilarating ways to occupy your time. But a few of your choir members will have needs that may take the edge off this joy, and you mustn't be surprised or disappointed by this. Many of them have an unusually strong need to belong to an accepting group. Choir is their family. Choir is the group that makes them feel good about themselves. They may have needs for approval, for activity, for interaction with others, for escape from a demanding job or a demanding home situation. You must be alert to these needs and try to relate to them in a helpful way. You must at times be a diplomat to steer situations away from conflict or hurt feelings. You must at times be a pastor or counselor to express concern for apparent crises or difficulties that come up in the lives of your singers.

Unlike most other groups, which bring together similar people, volunteer church choirs are usually made up of an unusually diverse group of people. Typically they are filled with persons of all ages, often teens to octogenarians. This cross-generation feature is a big plus for the church in many ways. But it also provides challenges for the director when selecting music or choosing social activities for the choir. The singers are married with their spouses in the choir, and they are married with their spouses at home—a very different situation. They are single because they want to be or they are single and don't want to be, and these are very different situations as well. They are employed. They are going to school. They are retired. Some are in the choir because this is the only group they belong to and have been in it fifty years. It is their life. Others are incredibly active people who do a hundred different things each week, and choir is simply one of the pleasant things they do, or their best escape from the trials of living.

Your singers are happy, confident people, well satisfied with their lives. They also are unhappy, resentful, difficult people who use their choir membership to act out hostilities and anxieties that are not appropriate in the setting you find them. They are people who differ in their politics, their values, their life situations, their aspirations, and their desires for the choir. Some want the choir to be a social group with parties every month. Some want choir to be all business. They don't have time for anything but the singing part. This is often a group of people who would not seek one another out in a crowded room for any ordinary social purpose. Put them all together and they have only one thing in common, a love of singing. At the moment they sing they are magically, even spiritually united by the music. Before and after this moment, they have very little reason to agree with one another about very much of anything or even to enjoy being together. Try to see behind their behavior. Never get drawn into the games they may want to play that are destructive. One of the most common games of this kind is called "the quit." If you as director do or say anything that offends the person, you will find out next week that he or she has quit the choir. You are then expected to call or visit the person to plead for forgiveness and beg for his or her return to the fold. Don't play a game like this. You can't win. Ignore the quit. It will be temporary. Unless, of course, you really did do something offensive.

As the director of the choir of many, many kinds of people, you are their common focus. You hold them together. You provide the common language and experience. They all relate to you, and you must be able to speak the language of each. You lead, arbitrate, direct, motivate, entertain, push, and energize. You organize them to do a common task, and to enjoy the experience and one another. It's a big job, but it's not impossible. If you enjoy them, are enthusiastic, fair, competent, organized, and fun to be with, they will respond. Being a director of a group of people who like working together is the greatest experience in the world. They will surround you with love, acceptance, and enthusiasm. But if you don't treat them with kindness and respect, you won't have any fun at all. And choir must be fun. I have heard choirs sing that are made up of people who don't enjoy being together, and I could hear the tension in the singing.

Enthusiasm is right up there in importance, and it must come from you. When rehearsal night comes, set aside your own needs for the evening and crank up as much enthusiasm as you can. It is contagious, and the truth is, the choir will reflect your attitude and manner as surely as your musical ability.

No matter how well you get along with the people in the choir, you need them, so let's talk about recruiting more members. The number one problem that most directors identify when they talk about their choirs is that they don't have enough members. Everybody wants more singers. How do we get more people to join the choir? If you have been directing a church choir for a few years, I finally got to your problem, right? Recruiting. You want me to give you some magical ideas for recruiting. OK, I have some. Have you got a pencil? You'll want to underline these ideas. They're for everyone. Some of them won't apply in your situation. Some of them might. This is everything I know about recruiting, so take what you want.

First, you need to let the congregation know that you would welcome some new members. Put a notice in the church newsletter and/or Sunday bulletin. Make it friendly and welcoming. Invite everyone to come and sing with you next Thursday at 7:30 P.M. You've already done this, I'll bet. And no one came. Well, of course no one came. If you expected this kind of invitation to bring new members, you haven't been working in the church very long. The purpose of this announcement wasn't to actually get new members, it was to let the congregation know that you would welcome some.

New choir members almost always have to be personally invited to join the choir. The best person to personally invite them is the director. You need to make phone calls. That's the most important recruiting idea that I have. Other choir members can do it too. That's second best, but still good. Personal invitations are needed. Keep a list of prospects in front of your members so they can work on people they know. Keep a list in front of you so you can mention choir to people that you meet in the church as you go to social and fellowship events.

But how do we identify choir prospects if they don't tell anyone they are singers? Here's how to develop a list. Start with everyone who has ever sung in the choir in the past. Talk to old-timers. Look through old programs. Keep a permanent list of anyone who has ever been a member. The reason he or she stopped being a member may be gone. The new baby may be in college now. The night job may have turned into a day job. The Wednesday night class may now be a Monday night class. Keep contacting former members. They can easily become current members. Ask the minister to set up some kind of procedure for finding out the interests and talents of new members when they join the church. The day someone joins a church is the day that he or she is most apt to be motivated to get involved. Have everyone who joins your church fill out some kind of talent survey. Be sure you get a copy of every survey that mentions music or choir. Now you have some more prospects.

Another way to identify prospects is to have an alumni choir Sunday once or twice a year. This is a day when you invite everyone in the church who used to sing in the choir, might some day want to sing in the choir, or always wished they could sing in the choir but are too busy, to come that Sunday morning an hour before the service. Practice one very familiar, old favorite anthem, like Stainer's "God So Loved the World," and do it that Sunday. You might be surprised how many people will show up. When they do, you have more prospects for future recruiting. Put them on your list. Sometimes just singing that one Sunday will spark an interest that will bring them back next week.

Or, how about an Easter choir? Announce that at the conclusion of the Easter service you will invite any and all singers to come to the front of the sanctuary and join in Handel's "Hallelujah Chorus." Borrow music from another church. Have one rehearsal thirty minutes before the service, and watch the people gather in large numbers to sing. Have a couple of choir members who know everybody quietly make a list of everyone who showed up. There you go. More people on your prospect list.

Another idea that I have used will involve some work, but surprisingly less than you might think. Prepare a musical survey of every person in the church. Make up a form on a single sheet of paper or a four-by-six-inch index card. Provide spaces to indicate every household member who has ever sung in a choir, including children and youth, what current conditions prevent choir membership, every member who plays a musical instrument, and anything else you think will be useful.

Say your church has 200 members. This may represent 125 households. Take out the forms for the present choir members, shut-ins, and people you are positive are not choir prospects. (Don't make any decisions for anyone, but if they live two states away they probably can't get to your rehearsals.) Now your stack of forms is down under a hundred. Ask ten of your choir members to make ten phone calls in the next three weeks and fill out the forms. You're all done. You have a file with every church family on a form that tells you which persons are singers. It even tells you why they aren't in the choir. Now get busy and invite the ones who have no excuse. When new people join the church, be sure to fill out a card for them.

Here's another idea that I've used, and it works too. Set a goal. Church people often shy away from setting goals, especially specific ones. But it is amazing to me how just setting a goal and making it public will put in motion the things that help the goal to be reached. Set the goal just high enough to sound difficult, but not so high that it is obviously unrealistic. Decide that you want seven new choir members by Christmas, which is two months away. Tell everyone: choir members, congregation—especially the congregation. You are going to have seven new choir members by Christmas. As soon as you tell everyone, it becomes other people's goal as well as yours. Watch. It will become the congregation's goal. People will help you recruit. It's amazing. You may not have to do a thing. It may just happen. You may not believe me, but try it anyway.

Here's a theory. You may not be able to do anything about this one, but I think it's an interesting theory. Who decided that your choir would have fifteen members, or twenty-three members, or twenty-eight members? I think the person who decided for many churches was the architect who designed the choir loft. The choir in the church where I work has never had more than an average of forty-two singers on Sunday mornings. Why? I think it's because there are forty-two seats in the choir loft. We've even had as many as sixty members, but we have never averaged more than forty-two. I think that the feeling that the loft is full works against you two ways. First, if the choir loft is full, the people in the congregation think the choir is big and you don't need any new members. If your choir loft seats fifteen, who says that's big? Maybe it's small. If there are forty-two in my church's choir loft we think the choir is big. But who says so? There is a church the same size as ours down the street with a choir of seventy-five. Maybe that's big. Its choir loft holds seventy-five. Does that make the choir big?

The other thing that works against you is that the choir members themselves think the choir is big. When they start thinking that, they don't feel very necessary. "Oh, you had a big choir Sunday, you didn't need me." That's a deadly feeling. If your singers ever start feeling that they aren't needed, you are in trouble. Change the definition of big. Keep telling people that fifteen is small, or twenty-three is small, or whatever number you have is small. You won't have a big choir until you get to twenty-five, or thirty, or fifty, or some other number that is bigger than your choir loft. The day you have to bring in extra chairs, or as in our case, have to have some choir members sit with the congregation and come to the loft for the anthem, is a great day. Tell your choir that the day you overflow your choir loft you will have a party. Keep some goodies in a closet, and the day it happens have a quick celebration after the service.

Choir growth depends on several very important things. The first requirement is that you must have a good choir before people will want to join it. That sounds a little like a chicken-and-egg problem. How can we have a good choir until we get more members? How can we get more members until we have a good choir? Well, work at it. Do what you do well, and do it with enthusiasm and smiling faces. That brings up the second requirement. The members of the choir must have fun and be excited about being together.

Nobody wants to join a marginally successful organization of people who don't seem to have a very good time together. Be successful in what you do. Have a good time doing it, and others will want to be a part of the fun. That's what I know about recruiting.

This chapter also is an appropriate place to mention the importance of your relationship with other persons in the church. There is an old adage among school teachers that the most important person to get along with in the school is the custodian. Like most adages this one contains a lot of truth. You must get along with the church custodian or your life will be miserable. He or she is one of your most helpful colleagues. Don't criticize this vital servant of the church. Don't complain about him or argue with him. I've found that if you help him set up chairs or carry music stands or whatever happens to be the job when you are around, he will respond well to someone who obviously respects what he does.

The church secretary is usually the person who holds the whole church together, and you will do well to have her or him on your side. Meet the deadlines that you are asked to meet for bulletin and newsletter information. Do whatever she asks, and she will be a priceless source of information and a willing producer of printed pages for you. Keep the secretary happy and you will be rewarded in many ways.

One of the program areas that sometimes experiences friction with the music program is Christian education. This won't be true for the adult choir as much as for the children's and youth choirs. The problems come from several directions. Both departments are program agencies that produce group activities primarily for members of the church. And thus, they often can be seen as competing for the same persons and for the same spaces in the church building and times on the calendar. Most problems between the two areas are calendar problems. If you want to avoid difficulty with the church school and the youth program, get together with the leaders and plan the calendar well ahead. Conflicts usually center around dates and spaces, and these can be solved much easier with careful advance planning.

I've left the most important person for last. Your relationship with the minister is a make-or-break issue for you as choir director. You must get along with him or her. Ministers come in all styles, with all degrees of knowledge and interest in music, and with all kinds of ideas about how music ought to fit into the worship of the church. If you want to keep your minister happy about your work, keep your choir members happy. When someone in the church has a complaint about you, the first place they go with their complaint is to the minister. Try to keep regular and open communication going with the minister, so that any problems that come up will find him or her with you trying to solve them instead of working with the problem person trying to solve you.

Share your plans, your dreams, your reasons for what you do, your problems, your successes with the minister, and you have a good chance of having support for your work. If you stay away, and let information, rumors, and opinions come to the pastor from other people first, you will not be in a good position when problems come up. There are two things that you must understand about the minister. First, he or she knows everything that happens, should happen, or is going to happen in the church. There is a large network of people who see to it that this is true. Second, the minister can win any debates or arguments with you if the issue is important enough. Be kind to your clergy colleague. Be patient. Keep the pastor informed and take suggestions from him or her as often as possible. There is no substitute for having a good working relationship with this person who is your boss.

Every person in the church is important to you. As you develop your relationships in the congregation, be as positive and enthusiastic as you possibly can with everyone. Love them, because they are the nicest people in the world, and they will return your good feelings in more ways than you can imagine.

CHAPTER NINE

TOMORROW YOU MUST GET ORGANIZED

If you are a choir director, you are an organizer. Whether you like it or not you are either primarily responsible, or at least very involved in, putting together the group life of the choir that you meet with twice a week. There are issues of schedule and activity that somebody has to guide, if not decide, and usually that person is the director.

An interesting dynamic is at work in church choirs. See if you think this is true. The larger the church (and choir), the more likely it is that the director alone determines how the group will be organized. He or she is more likely to be a paid professional church musician, and is given the responsibility and the permission to make decisions about most things, musical or otherwise. The smaller the church, the more likely that choir officers or a committee of some kind will make decisions about most of the nonmusical organization. We're talking here about parties, money raising, rules and regulations, dues, robe care, music library, flowers for sickness and death in the choir's extended family—all the nitty-gritty details that have little to do with making music. Regardless of the size of your church, one way or another, you as the director will be involved in all of this. How organized do you want the choir to be? Will there be rules about attendance, dress, and deportment? Will there be parties every month or so? Will there be regular meetings of choir officers? Will these people make decisions about the choir's work as well as its play?

How about extra concerts? Will the choir do cantatas during Advent and Lent? Will these need to be advertised? Who will make arrangements for ushers and child care? Who decides about the summer? Will the choir sing all summer? Will you do a secular concert in the spring to raise money? Will this require tickets to be sold? Should there be a committee for publicity? Will the choir have its own money? Does it need a treasurer and a bank account? What about robes? Who buys the robes? Who takes care of them, assigning a robe to each member, arranging for cleaning and repair?

This is all organizational stuff that somebody has to do. I've asked a lot of questions. I suppose you're thinking that I'm going to answer them in this chapter, right? Well, I'm not. I can't answer them for your situation, but I can raise them so that you will give them some thought and add some ideas that might help you to get your choir's act together if it isn't already. The first suggestion, I guess, is the same I have made before. Let it all happen the way it has happened before for a while. But if you are going to be at it for very long, you'll be called on to make some suggestions, if not decisions, before long. Let's start with rules.

The first rule for rules is to have very few, as few as possible. An example of a rule would be that if you miss two rehearsals in a row, you can't sing on Sunday. That's a common one. But in many situations it isn't very workable. Like most rules, its purpose is to fall on the line between two positions held by different people, in this case those who think the choir should take all the help it can get on Sunday and those who think it isn't fair to be able to sing if you haven't been in rehearsals. It comes down at the point of what to do when Fred and Mary, who used to sing in the choir, come back for one Sunday to visit. Do they sing, even though they weren't at rehearsal? How about George who was just moved to the second shift at his job, and can't make rehearsals at all. Can he still sing Sundays if he "knows" the music?

You'll find at least two distinct attitudes toward all this, and you probably have one of your own. Maybe the line can be drawn between a one-time thing, such as visiting musicians who want to sing with the choir while they are in town, and the person who can't ever get to rehearsals. What about the college students who come home for Christmas Sunday or Easter, but not in time for rehearsals? It's never easy. If you have a rule, you'll have situations where you or somebody will want to make an exception. Maybe you can cast it in the form of a guideline rather than a rule. Maybe you don't have strong feelings. But somebody might, so be careful. The worst thing that can happen is that you regularly approve of people sitting in on Sunday while several choir members are real unhappy about it. Here's an underlying principle that might be a good guide for you when you are considering rules of any kind. In the church, the purpose for rules is to protect the feelings of the people involved. Check out what the people's feelings are, get a group decision about it, and then set up your procedures and practices to fit.

Now for some basic choir organization things. Some of these you will want to do, some you will not. Every director must decide how organized to be. Believe it or not, it's real easy to be too organized. For instance, it is possible to arrange the music library with an elaborate system of numbers and card files that takes more time managing than it is worth. You have to find a level that fits for you and the church. The simplest library system probably involves a number for each anthem without regard to any alphabetizing as far as the storage is concerned. If the church has several choirs, maybe the adult choir anthems could be numbered from one. The children's choir music would start at 1,000, youth choir 2,000, Christmas music 3,000, Lent and Easter, 4,000, or something like that. Do your alphabetizing in a card file. Each anthem could have two cards, one beginning with the title and one with the composer. Note on the card how many copies there are, when the music was purchased, whether there are parts for soloists or instrumentalists. But remember, the more complicated you make everything, the more maintenance it will require. The important thing is to do it carefully and keep it up-to-date.

Every choir member needs his or her own folder. Get the type that will hold a pencil. Encourage singers to mark their music during rehearsals. They should indicate phrasing, important expression and tempo marks, difficult notes, accidentals, and other surprises in the music as you suggest them. This will save time and help the singers to remember your instructions between rehearsals. And it will ensure that everyone will get the same piece of music each week. Otherwise, the marks that a singer made this week won't be any help next week.

You also need a system for passing out new music and supplying previously distributed music to those who don't have copies. A good way is to have the new music for the evening on a table just inside the door so people can pick it up as they come in. Extra copies of previously distributed music should be in a different place. Singers should come in the room, pick up new music, look at the board for the list of what is needed at rehearsal and then pick up anything that they don't have before they sit down. There also should be an obvious place to put music that the choir is finished with. Passing out and collecting music can be a big time waster. Be sure you have a system that takes as little time as possible.

It's also very helpful for everybody if you put together a choir roster and run off copies for all choir members. The first thing this does is help the people get acquainted with one another. As soon as the membership has been established for the year (maybe by October), put together a list of the singers by sections. Include each person's address and phone number, birthday and occupation. This helps communication when it comes to telephoning, or car pooling or even sending Christmas cards. The next step in this kind of choir communication is to have a monthly newsletter. This doesn't take much planning and effort if some choir members can help, and it is worth it. Include the names of the anthems that will be sung during the month. Include any dates that you want your singers to keep in mind. Include thank-you's to those who have helped the choir in some individual way. Include a list of those who have had perfect attendance or who were present or accounted for every Sunday last month. This is your opportunity to keep your choir members informed. It will help them to feel a part of what is happening musically in the church. It will help them to plan their personal schedules around that of the choir.

Here's a good way to start your choir year. Have a beginning-of-the-year retreat. The Saturday before the first Sunday that you sing is a good day. Find a place that will provide a reasonably good rehearsal setting, some opportunities for recreation, and a place for the group to eat. A camp or a lodge can be ideal. If one of the members of the church has a large cottage on a lake, that might be ideal. It is important to get away from the church. You will need a place where your singers can work and play together for as long as possible. The retreat might start with coffee at 10:00 A.M. and a good, long rehearsal. Sack lunches could be brought by the choir members themselves. After lunch, have some fun together and then have another rehearsal in the middle of the afternoon. This one should include the introduction of your Christmas music or some other big project.

Follow the second rehearsal with a business meeting. At this time you can introduce new members, go over the choir procedures, elect officers, and have the minister say a few kind words. Then spend some time as director giving the choir a preview of your plans and goals for the entire year. Conclude with supper and perhaps a brief worship service. You can accomplish enough in one day to start right out the next day with a well-prepared choir. And the singers will have worked and played together for a day, a good way to build some new friendships and get the year started off right.

How about parties? Should you have them often or just once or twice a year? How important is the social aspect of the choir's activities? Here's one to leave up to the choir members themselves. From your standpoint, congeniality and morale are very important. A choir that is made up of people who enjoy one another and get along well will sing much better than one that doesn't. Let the choir discuss its social life and plan it too.

There are lots more details that you'll have to look at sooner or later. There's money. There may not be much, but the choir needs money. Maybe you should have two or three dollars a year dues, which could go for flowers when people have illnesses or deaths in the family. The choir certainly shouldn't have to buy its own music. That is an allchurch budget (worship committee or music committee) responsibility. I don't even think it should have to buy its own robes, but I know of situations where choirs do raise money for this.

You probably will have to deal with robes or vestments of some kind. This is pure busywork, and you need a robe person or committee to do it all. Remember, you're new. You may not be a good organizer. You may not be a good delegator of responsibility. Appoint choir officers, and assign to them the items in this area that you can't get a handle on. Tell them diplomatically and apologetically that you don't have time to worry about all this stuff. The officers will be glad to do things if they see that they aren't appropriate for you and if they are given permission to make the decisions about these areas. Can you give up having control over things like rules or parties? If you want to make all the decisions, be prepared to do many more things yourself than if you are willing to let the choir members decide things. The best idea is to save your energies for those things that really require your attention.

Being organized is important for a choir director. You need to find a balance between being so compulsive about details that they get in everyone's way and take up too much time and energy (both in talking about them and doing them), and not being organized enough so that people don't know what is happening or how they can help. There's a fine line between these extremes. Once you find it, stay on it. You need to get organized so you can think about important things like singing.

CHAPTER TEN

WHAT'S A CHOIR FOR?

W hy do we have a choir, anyway? What kind of a question is that? Every church has a choir. We have to have a choir. Imagine a church without a choir. Have you ever known of a church that didn't have a choir? Impossible. It would be unchristian, unpatriotic, unthinkable. Or is it? Is it really necessary to go to all the effort to organize and rehearse a choir each week? Shouldn't there at least be a standard of quality or size or something? Some churches have a choir even when the choir isn't very good. Can you imagine that? Why do we have choirs, anyway? There must be some pretty strong reasons. What are they?

Here is a place where it might be instructive to observe a church that doesn't have a choir to see why its congregation feels the need for one. A newly organized church that is starting everything from scratch or a small church that lacks leadership or does not have enough people interested in singing may not have a choir for a time. What is the impulse in churches that demands that they have a choir? Listen to a pastor who is in the process of starting a choir where there isn't one. Usually he or she begins by talking about the congregational singing.

Probably the first reason for having a choir, and it certainly is the most important one, is to lead and encourage the congregation in its singing. Let's not go another step back and question the need for congregational singing. That's another book. We have to start somewhere. This emphasis on leading hymn singing isn't very glamorous, and choir members don't think about it very much. They are more apt to think of themselves as singing for the congregation to listen, and that's certainly appropriate too. We'll get to that in a minute. But remind your people from time to time that they are first in their places on Sunday to lead the people in singing. If the best reason for having a choir is to support and lead the congregation in its participation in worship, the choir then becomes a part of the worship leadership and at the same time a part of the congregation.

Now as long as the musicians are there, they might as well sing by themselves too. Here comes the other stuff. When the choir does sing, its role has two main directions. Sometimes, depending on the text of the anthem, it is singing words of devotion or exhortation to the congregation. Ordinarily, these words should be scriptural or written by someone who is a sound theologian. The words are enhanced and made more expressive and more powerful by the music and the singing voices for the edification of the members of the congregation. Other times, the choir is singing a prayer addressed to God on behalf of the congregation, using the music and the singing voices to make the prayer more beautiful and impassioned, if not more worthy. The choir, then, stands in the middle, sometimes acting as worship leader, sometime acting as representative of the congregation.

So, if these are the functions of the choir, what about the feeling that what musicians do in worship is really just entertainment? Oh, you say, nobody feels that way. Think about it. How readily does your congregation applaud the musicians who sing for it? Is applause really appropriate? Can you imagine applauding the minister when he or she finishes praying or reading the scripture? What is the difference? It might have been a very fine prayer or reading, delivered beautifully in a rich, reverent voice. On the other hand, what does a group of people do when it feels moved by some beautiful music? It's only natural to want to applaud. There's a fine line between the natural and spontaneous reaction of a congregation to an unusually meaningful presentation and the weekly , thoughtless applause for musical presentations, no matter how perfunctory. And if we are only going to applaud the good Sundays, or just the children or youth when they sing, how do we decide what is worthy of applause and what isn't? This can get complicated. To be sure, there are only two ways a group of people can demonstrate its approval or disapproval for something, to clap or to boo, but to cheer for a prayer sung by someone on your behalf certainly seems inappropriate.

Unfortunately these days, our teacher in these matters often is television. Some of our worst ideas about music and worship come from watching religious television programs. Most of this kind of T.V. programming is the product of a pretty specific theological viewpoint and practice, and what might be valid and helpful for those persons is not necessarily valid and helpful for all Christian congregations. Most of what we see on television is also the product of organizations led by big-name evangelists who tailor the half-hour or hour program for its greatest impact on the listener sitting at home. What this means for the most part is two things—a powerful, evangelistic, spoken message surrounded by entertainment-like music sung by soloists or small groups. It is nearly impossible to include in a television worship experience what is the most important kind of church music, that which is sung by the worshipers themselves. Worship is primarily something we do rather than something we watch specialists do on television or in our own church. This is a very important point for anyone leading in worship or directing a group that leads in worship.

A musician's work is filled with ego and personal effort and all of the things that make the performer vulnerable to criticism and praise. Praise for a fine contribution to worship is not inappropriate, but the temptation for the musician is certainly always present to let the performance be a chance to gather personal glory for one's offering of talent. Again, this is a fine line, and all of us live and sing and play on that line.

There are other reasons for having a choir. When asked why their church has a choir, many people would list the function of the choir as an outlet for the talent and service of the singers. Others would talk about how the choir is a way of getting people involved in their church. Others would talk about the arts themselves and the beauty they bring to worship and the outlet for creativity that is so appropriate among our offerings to our Creator.

You can think of other reasons for having a choir, I'm sure. The purpose of this chapter is primarily to ask the questions that will stir your thinking. The important thing, I think, is to avoid thinking about your work as a musician in the church as just another job, or just another way to exercise your hobby, singing. I know professional musicians who have "church jobs," which are just another way for them to use their training and talent to make money. They can do their thing in any denomination. Whether they have compatible beliefs with their employers or not isn't important to them. If there is any argument here about whether this is appropriate, I guess I'd come down on the side of those who believe that a leader of worship probably ought to believe what he or she is saying or singing.

Thoughtful reflection about what you do as a leader in the church is always healthy. Reflection about what kind of music you produce and how you produce it is too. Is it important to do "good" music, as opposed to "bad" music, in the church? What makes some music "good" and some "bad"? Shall we tackle this one, or is that another book too? For me, good music is music that meets some pretty specific criteria. I think the music that I sing or that the choir I lead sings ought to have a text that I can believe. The mention of God or Jesus in an anthem isn't enough for me to decide it is appropriate. Actually, the text is where I always begin when choosing anthems for the choir. Are the words scriptural? If not, do they say anything, and do they say it well? Is it good poetry? Do the words reflect the theological concepts and emphases that the congregation hears from the pulpit? Do we really think we should sing about things that are not consistent with the prevailing theological understandings of the congregation? I'm not going to get specific here because my examples would probably not fit your situation. But think about it as you read the text of your anthems. Can you imagine your minister saying those words in a sermon?

The other test for the text is more difficult. Does the anthem say what it says in some fresh or dramatic or inspirational or powerful way? Or are the words a series of churchy clichés that are squeezed and twisted and contrived to follow someone's rhyming dictionary? The poetic art is as difficult and elusive as the compositional one. Many of the new anthems that I look at every year are obviously written by a musician who is moderately clever with words, but has nothing of real value to say.

And then there is the music. Every time we select an anthem or a hymn for the choir to sing we make a judgment about the music involved. What makes the choice of music appropriate in some churches and less than appropriate in others? If I don't talk about my personal preferences and the aesthetic convictions that come out of my musical training, I am left with two ideas. The first has to do with variety. One of the fundamental characteristics of our society and of the church, at least the kind of church in which I serve, is plurality or diversity or variety among the people. Just a variety of age groups will produce a wide variety of musical responses among the people. And that is just the beginning. There is ethnic and cultural and racial diversity. There is theological diversity. There is diversity of background, even within one denomination. The music that is used in the worship of most churches these days must be of a wide variety of style. As the choir director, you must never think of the worship of your church as your worship. It belongs to the congregation, which is made up of a large number of different kinds of people. If all of the music you choose is of the same type and style, you are not serving your congregation or your choir well.

The second criterion I have is much more difficult to describe or identify and is clearly subjective in some respects. I think most of the music we use in the church should be "good" enough to keep its welcome over a long period of time. The ultimate test of good music is whether it becomes more attractive and effective as the singer or listener gets to know it, or wears out its welcome with repeated use. Your responsibility as the trained musician is to be a better predictor of this phenomenon than the average person. Theoretically, you have some basis on which to predict whether a piece of music is worthy of being added to the repertoire of the choir and its permanent library.

If you are just starting out as a choir director, all of the questions in this chapter are probably pretty heady for you. You may not want to deal with them right now. If so, let someone else worry about them for a while. Your own philosophy about your work will emerge as you think about the place and purpose of music in the church. Just be sure that you do think about them sometime. Music without clear purpose and thoughtful planning contributes little to the worship of God in any church.

CHAPTER ELEVEN

NOW DO IT—WEEK AFTER WEEK AFTER WEEK

Now it's time to settle in for the long haul. The hard part is that it happens every week, whether you are ready or not. This chapter is about what it takes to do it and do it and do it and do it. There will be good rehearsals and bad rehearsals, good Sundays and bad Sundays. You will like your choice of music some Sundays and hate it some Sundays. You will have everyone in place some Sundays and half the choir sick or out of town some Sundays. Church music is a hazardous pursuit. You'll get discouraged. You'll be thrilled with the progress. You'll wonder why you're doing it. It will be up and down. If you can be up more than down, you're doing fine. Let's try to deal with the overall ideas that will keep you going through it all. Here's where I give you the broad generalizations, the overall rules and regulations, the suggestions and advice on how to just cope.

The hardest thing about church music is that musicians have to produce something new every seven days. Very few other musicians have to be so productive. Those who do are professionals and have resources, like money to spend, to help them do it. Most church music is made by volunteer amateurs, sometimes led by semi-paid or volunteer, semi-trained directors. And they must produce music for public hearing every Sunday at least once, and sometimes twice. And to compound the problem, the listeners in the pew have developed very high standards of music appreciation and discrimination because they hear the best music in the world, performed by the best musicians in the world, right in their own living rooms on television, radio, and recordings. Like it or not, we in the church are competing with the best. As the director of a volunteer church choir, you have been asked to come up with something sung by an ever-changing combination of singers of a wide variety of ability week after week after week. And these singers may or may not even come regularly on rehearsal nights or Sundays. Even school groups get to work six or eight weeks, often with daily rehearsals, for one concert. You and I have to produce next Sunday, ready or not.

Most of this book has been about the musical, technical aspects of being a choir director. Most of it has been ideas for specific things you can do to do the job better. This final chapter will begin with a look at the basic idea of leadership itself and what it takes to keep going year after year. Surely you realize that musicianship is just one of the requirements for your new responsibility. A church choir director will be successful or unsuccessful for her or his leadership skills, as well as for musical skills. It's not enough to just be a good musician, as demanding as that is. A church choir director must be a conductor, a coach, a teacher, a pastor, a dictator, a diplomat, a salesperson, a promoter, a cheerleader, a caregiver, a people person, an idea person, an organizer, a singer, and oh yes, a musician.

You can do all of the rest, but if you aren't a diplomat or a caregiver or a teacher you probably won't do very well in the church. Patience may be the most important character trait of all for the church choir director. Or compassion. Or diplomacy. Remember, your singers are volunteers who simply will not come if the experience isn't fun or satisfying to them. It's absolutely necessary that you have an accepting attitude toward your singers. You may encounter one who demands your attention because he or she doesn't get attention from anyone else. You may have a singer who is angry or depressed or lonely or insecure, and he or she comes to choir looking for a place to express some of this or get acceptance or relief from it.

Early in your career as a church choir director, whether it lasts two months or two decades, you will have to decide which is more important, the music that your choir produces or the needs of the individual members, some of which have nothing to do with singing. If you don't decide in favor of the individual persons in your choir, you will not be successful. It's impossible to overemphasize the importance of being able to get along with them. Leadership involves being able to rise above the normal reactions that you might have to a difficult person or group. You are responsible for the progress of the group as a whole, and you have to let your own needs go for the greater good.

Leadership also involves being prepared for the rehearsal, and thinking ahead all the time about where the work of the choir is going. It involves enthusiasm, humor, wisdom, concern for persons, foresight, competence in the musical skills required, and a continuous supply of new ideas. Where does one get training in this kind of leadership? Do you have to go to college? What if you don't have the time, the money, or the inclination to go to college? Well, guess what? You don't have to go to college. There is a way to get training, in some ways better and more practical training than you get in college, in a fraction of the time and expense. Weeklong summer workshops are held throughout the country that will give you intense and directly practical training and experience to help you in your work in church music. Given the fact that you have basic musical training and skills (like conducting and voice training), the ideas, information, resources, training, and inspiration that can come from one or two weeklong workshops each year will probably be more beneficial than most college programs. These are sponsored by denominational musicians' organizations, independent church music organizations, colleges, and other religious and educational institutions. My college and graduate school training in music didn't teach me a single thing about working with volunteer singers, planning music for worship, getting along with ministers, recruiting new choir members, and all the other church things that I have to do. Find out where the workshops are and talk your church into paying your expenses. It will be worth it in new music and ideas alone.

Beyond getting some good, practical training, there are some other things you can do that will help your credibility, if not your popularity, with the congregation. Get involved in things that have nothing to do with the choir. Go to church dinners, Bible studies, fellowship events, anywhere that people gather. Make the most of informal settings like the after-church coffee or the reception for new members. Be visible. Introduce yourself wherever you go. The church members will appreciate having a choir director who is interested in the church and cares about its program. If you really want to nail this down, volunteer for an ongoing responsibility that has nothing to do with directing the choir. Help serve dinners or train the acolytes or organize parties or teach a church school class. If the church members see you making a nonmusical contribution, they will support your musical efforts more enthusiastically. All this will help you get to know the members of the church who just might join the choir sometime. You need to keep in touch with prospective members, wherever they are, and the better you know the congregation, the easier this will be.

A good choir director is a teacher. You will encounter poor singers in your choir. You don't believe that a poor adult singer has to stay a poor adult singer, do you? Do you believe adults can learn to sing better or do you categorize people as good or bad musicians and accept that for all time? Isn't it more helpful to see your job as a teaching one? If you have a choir member who cannot sing well, or can't read music well, get busy and teach him or her. He'll be grateful, and so will the choir.

A good choir director is a promoter. You have to sell your program if you want the congregation to support it and singers to join the choir. Enthusiasm and energy must be evident in everything you do. You must be excited about the choir and its singing. This is the first step in gaining support for your work. Then you must communicate what you are doing to the congregation and sell your new ideas to both the choir and the people in the pew. Go to business meetings and social functions of the church and talk about the choir every chance you get.

Obviously, a good choir director is also a good musician. A good musician works at improving his or her musicianship constantly. It's important that you don't just stand back and tell others how to make music without thinking about your own abilities. You must be learning and improving too. What can you do to improve your own skills? Your ear is your greatest asset. Listen, listen, listen. Listen to choral music sung by outstanding choirs. This means attending live concerts whenever possible and listening to recordings the rest of the time. You need an aural picture in your head of good choral sound. This will give you something to work toward with your own choir. Improving your ear also means sharpening it as a critical tool. Anything you can do to improve your discriminating ear will be beneficial. For instance, if you have a personal computer, buy yourself an ear training program that is used in music theory classes. There are some outstanding ones available. A few minutes a day with one of these, and you will improve your ear dramatically.

How are your piano skills? If you don't play the piano, take some lessons. There is a huge advantage to being able to play over choir music to select it and to prepare your rehearsals with the choir. Or, how about some voice lessons? There is no end to your training. The pursuit of musical excellence as a performer or conductor is a lifetime job, and the payoff for efforts in self-improvement is enormous.

To be a church choir director week after week takes a certain kind of personal stability that will keep you on an even keel in spite of people problems that may crop up. You will need a big reserve of enthusiasm and energy that will keep you out in front of your choir, leading the way toward constant improvement and growth in spite of temporary setbacks that inevitably happen. A choir is like a sports team, needing constant motivation and inspiration to keep the emotions high and the energy going. Maybe enthusiasm is the most important thing. For every ounce of enthusiasm that you communicate to your singers you will receive pounds of reward as they sing to please you and are grateful to you for what you help them discover and express in the music. Directing a church choir week after week can provide the fuel that keeps you going as you share with eager musicians the love of good singing and the satisfaction of serving the church. Be grateful that

Sundays come by regularly, even if you don't always feel ready for them. Think of each of your meetings with your choir as an important boost to your own feelings of goodwill and a vital part of your own growth in the faith, and you will gain from the experience much more than you can possibly give, week after week after week.

I hope that these eleven chapters of more or less organized and disorganized ideas about directing a church choir have been helpful to you as you direct the choir in your church. I hope that I have adequately conveyed my enthusiasm for the incomparable joy and privilege it is to be in this position. Singers are a continual pleasure to work with if they are treated with kindness and enthusiasm. You have been selected to stand in front of the finest people in your congregation, and you will do just fine. Wave your arms at them. Smile as they sing. Smile when they are done, and love each one of them. The love will come back to you multiplied by the number of sopranos, altos, tenors, and basses that you have singing for you. Be confident. Be positive. Be enthusiastic. Be ambitious. Be resourceful. Be conscientious. Be continually learning and growing yourself, and you will be rewarded beyond your imagination.